# Super Easy Vegan
# Slow Cooker Cookbook

# SUPER EASY VEGAN

## Slow Cooker Cookbook

**100+** EASY, HEALTHY RECIPES
THAT ARE READY WHEN YOU ARE

Toni Okamoto

**ROCKRIDGE
PRESS**

*To my parents, George and Lisa Okamoto, who worked 40 to 60 hours per week and took night classes, while raising three very active kids, and still managed to have a warm meal on the table for us every night. Thank you and I love you.*

# CONTENTS

Quick Fix Lentil Tacos (page 25)

# INTRODUCTION

You would think that because I've spent my career teaching people how to make plant-based meals, I'd be very passionate about cooking. The truth is, my favorite part about cooking is eating, and if I can make my meals with the least amount of time, effort, and dirty dishes, the food itself becomes even more enjoyable. That's why slow cookers are the only kitchen appliance I regularly recommend. A slow cooker can get healthier, plant-based foods into your life that are delicious, inexpensive, and very convenient. Cook dried beans overnight while you sleep, add veggies and chili spices before you go to work, and when your day is done, you'll arrive to a home filled with mouthwatering aromas and a comforting meal. It doesn't get much easier than that!

As you'll discover while reading *Super Easy Vegan Slow Cooker Cookbook,* gone are the days of using a 1970s-era burnt orange or avocado green Crock Pot to figure out how you'll salvage inexpensive tough cuts of meat. Instead, spend the least amount of time in the kitchen while still serving a flavorful, creative, nutritious meal for dinner. I'll show you how to maximize your food budget and use your time in the kitchen efficiently by keeping all recipe prep times under 15 minutes, as well as give you some ideas for how to plan your weekly menus wisely.

The recipes in this book are designed for people like me who love eating delicious things but don't love complicated cooking or doing massive amounts of dishes. These recipes are for busy people who want to feed themselves and their families nourishing food without spending a fortune, and who want to focus on whole foods instead of packaged or processed. If that sounds like you, get ready to have stress-free evenings without scurrying home to start dinner. Begin planning what you're going to do with all the time you'll save by making super easy vegan meals in your slow cooker.

# CHAPTER ONE

# LET'S KEEP THIS BRIEF

We all want to eat healthy for less—less time, less money, less effort. Using a slow cooker to make your meals helps with all of that. Prep ingredients in under 15 minutes while cleaning out your pantry in the process. Sit back and enjoy life as your slow cooker does the work for you.

## Whole Foods, Fast and Slow

My goal with this book is to help you spend the least amount of time and energy in the kitchen, while still serving yourself and your family delicious and nutritious meals. To cut some corners on time, I'm going to suggest using convenient ingredients like frozen produce and canned beans. When I first began cooking often, I was concerned about the freshness and lower nutritional value of pre-prepped ingredients. But when the realistic alternative to pre-prepped food turned out to be eating fast food or microwaved meals because I had no extra time during my week, I realized that pre-prepped was by far the better option. I now see it as a way to get the nutrition you need without the hassle.

If you prefer using homemade beans and fresh produce, that's totally fine. The recipes I provide are designed to keep prep time to a minimum, but all the recipes are flexible and easily modified. Just make sure to budget extra time for cooking and prep if you're using different ingredients.

Even though I'll be providing you with many cooking shortcuts, I will not ask you to purchase a bunch of premade sauces or canned soups. *The Super Easy Vegan Slow Cooker Cookbook* sticks to plant-based foods that are healthy, nourishing, and considerate of your time and money. The food will be so familiar and comforting that even your most skeptical omnivorous friend will enjoy it.

## Easy Does It

Many people believe that adopting a plant-based diet means having to eat salad every day. That's not the case at all! "Plant-based" means not eating meat, fish, dairy, or eggs, which is absolutely possible to do while still cooking in a manner that's familiar, flavorful, and convenient. The biggest difference is that you're now choosing a diet that is naturally cholesterol-free, lower in calories and fat, and generally more nutritious, since meals are always packed with produce. When you cook healthy, plant-based foods in a fashion that saves you time and energy, you truly maximize your time in the kitchen.

## Cook Smarter

Planning ahead is important for maximizing the efficiency of your slow cooker. I recommend using your day off to choose your recipes for the week, make a list of ingredients you need, do your grocery shopping, and start your prep work. When considering what you'd like to make, keep in mind what you already have in your pantry and refrigerator. Slow cookers are a great way to minimize food waste and use produce that may be on its way out. Think of the recipes in this cookbook as a flexible guide to inspire your creativity. If the recipe calls for kale when you have spinach, or for frozen butternut squash when you only have a fresh one, feel free to make substitutions so you don't have to unnecessarily purchase more ingredients.

Even when I have the best intentions to make a healthy meal midweek, that goal becomes less realistic when I'm working and going to school full time. To ensure that I'm continuing to eat well all week long, I use my day off to cut veggies. I throw the chopped produce in a storage container with all the other ingredients for my meal, and when things become hectic, my dinner is one less thing that requires my energy. All I have to do is tip my recipe ingredients and prechopped veggies into my slow cooker, and boom—dinner is in the works.

## Smart Shopping

Take the meal-prep fast track by purchasing ingredients that make your life easier. In addition to keeping your pantry stocked with bulk dry ingredients and canned items, I recommend shopping for precut and prewashed veggies to save even more time and energy. When doing this, I assess what is most important for me to save. If I want to save money, I look for the cheapest produce and prep it all on my day off. If I want to save time, I'll spend a bit more money for the convenience of pre-prepped ingredients.

Since I use garlic in nearly every savory recipe, I keep jarred, minced garlic in my refrigerator. It's cheap, you get a large quantity, and it saves you tons of time. I highly recommend doing this. Other ingredients that save on time without costing much more include bags of baby kale or spinach, frozen diced onions, frozen greens, frozen broccoli, and frozen chopped carrots.

# 10 Ingredients to Have on Hand

A well-stocked kitchen can make your life extra easy—these are the items I go to again and again when creating meals.

**BEANS:** You can easily make these inexpensive sources of protein from scratch in a slow cooker or buy them in cans to throw in chili, soups, and more. I usually have at least a couple cans of pintos, garbanzos, and black beans in my pantry, plus an assortment of dried beans.

**GREENS:** Slow-cooked meals are so packed with flavor, children don't even realize their food is filled with kale, spinach, or collards.

**FROZEN VEGGIES:** When they're frozen instead of fresh, you don't have to worry about using them quickly or chopping them up.

**ONIONS AND GARLIC:** They form the foundation of almost every savory dish I make.

**GRAINS:** Rice, barley, and (although it's not technically a grain) quinoa are all good to have at the ready.

**SPICES:** You can find spices that are less expensive by shopping at international markets or buying in bulk. I always keep cumin, chili powder, black pepper, red pepper flakes, and oregano in my spice cupboard.

**CANNED TOMATOES:** I enjoy tomatoes, so I stay stocked up on canned tomato sauce, diced tomatoes, and tomato paste.

**LENTILS:** Another easy and inexpensive protein option. I add these to soups, salads, and one-pot meals.

**POTATOES:** Is there anything potatoes aren't good in? They're an inexpensive, filling, comforting ingredient for soups and curries.

**VEGETABLE BROTH:** Whether in a can, carton, jar, or as bouillon cubes (I recommend the Edward & Sons cubes), broth is indispensable. To make your own, try my Very Easy Vegetable Broth (page 14).

## Top It Off

Cooking is one of my biggest creative outlets. It allows me to feel artistic in the most gratifying way, because when I'm done with my masterpiece, I get to eat it up. I explore this further by being generous with garnishes and toppings, especially hot sauce. I love Valentina, Cholula, sriracha, Tapatío, and any other condiment that will provide a kick to my food. I keep barbecue sauce, Just Mayo vegan sriracha mayo, sweet chili sauce, soy sauce, and more stocked in my pantry in case I'm feeling inspired to try new pairings. I recommend sticking to things you know will complement your dish. For example, when serving chili, pair it with a dollop of guacamole or some salsa. In chapter 5, I'll set you up with some great options, including homemade guacamole and salsa and a delicious cashew cream.

## About the Recipes

You'll notice that the recipes in chapters 2 and 3 are broken up in a different format than those in the rest of the book. Here's how it works: In chapter 2, the unbeatable basic recipe is followed by two variations that incorporate the basic ingredients. For example, you'll learn how to make Basic Beans—a standard, go-to beans recipe that works in a ton of recipes—as well as a Quinoa-and-Bean Salad and Chana Masala, two recipes that incorporate the beans. In chapter 3, we again have main recipes, and then one variation that mixes up the flavor profile a bit and one super simple salad that comes together in 15 minutes and pairs really well with the main recipe. When the slow cooker is making the main, tossing together a quick side salad means that dinner is ready in no time! Chapters 4 and 5 have straightforward, stand-alone recipes for complete one-pot meals as well as go-to staples for sauces and toppings that will bring your slow-cooked dishes to life. When creating these recipes, I used a 4-quart slow cooker, but have indicated if the recipe requires a 6-quart. Of course, the recipes were all created with your budget in mind!

Lazy Lentils (page 24)

# UNBEATABLE BASICS

# BASIC BEANS

Beans are one of the most versatile and inexpensive staples you can make in a slow cooker. You can make them plain, like in this recipe, or you can follow my tips to dress them up. They can be a side, the base of a salad, used in a soup or chili, flavored with Tex-Mex or Indian spices . . . the possibilities are endless. SERVINGS: 6

GLUTEN-FREE
SOY-FREE
NUT-FREE
BUDGET-FRIENDLY

**1 pound dry beans
(any type), rinsed
Enough water to cover the
beans in your slow cooker
by about 2 inches**

PREP TIME: 10 MINUTES
COOK TIME: 6 TO 8 HOURS

Add beans and water to your slow cooker and cook on low for 6 to 8 hours.

**WARNING:** If you're cooking kidney beans, you must boil them for 10 minutes before cooking. This neutralizes a toxin called phytohemagglutinin which is uncomfortable to consume.

**COOKING TIP:** If you like your beans on the firm side, give them a taste at 6 hours to see if they're at your desired consistency.

**INGREDIENT VARIATION:** You can switch it up every time you make your beans by adding a handful of diced onion, 1 tablespoon minced garlic, 2 bay leaves, or different spices.

**PER SERVING:** Calories: 255; Total fat: <1g; Protein: 17g; Sodium: 9mg; Fiber: 12g

# QUINOA-AND-BEAN SALAD

VARIATION ON BASIC BEANS

This meal is quick to whip up and extremely adaptable. You can add a handful of fresh corn kernels, ½ teaspoon ground cumin, some grilled zucchini, and anything else you can think of. Make it your own! **SERVINGS: 2**

GLUTEN-FREE
SOY-FREE
NUT-FREE
BUDGET-FRIENDLY

Scant 2 cups Very Easy
    Vegetable Broth (page 14)
    or store bought
1 cup uncooked quinoa, rinsed
Pinch salt, plus more for
    seasoning
¾ cup your choice
    cooked beans
1 avocado, pitted, peeled, and
    diced into bite-size pieces
⅛ cup diced red onion
Handful cherry
    tomatoes, halved
Juice of ½ lime
Freshly ground black pepper
Dash hot sauce (optional)

PREP TIME: 10 MINUTES
COOK TIME: 20 MINUTES
TOTAL TIME: 40 MINUTES

1.  Bring the vegetable broth to a boil, then add the quinoa and the pinch of salt.

2.  Cover, reduce the heat to low, and cook for 20 minutes. Let stand, covered, for 5 minutes, then transfer to a large bowl to cool completely.

3.  Add the beans, avocado, red onion, cherry tomatoes, and lime juice to the cooled quinoa. Season with salt and pepper, and hot sauce (if using). Mix thoroughly.

**INGREDIENT TIP:** Save time by purchasing packaged, precooked quinoa, or make a big batch of quinoa on your day off to use throughout the week.

**INGREDIENT VARIATION:** Try making this with couscous or Israeli couscous instead of quinoa. Use any type of tomatoes you have on hand—just dice them up and throw them in.

**LOVE YOUR LEFTOVERS:** This is a protein-packed, filling salad. If you'd like to save some for tomorrow, it tastes great served as a side to a sandwich.

**PER SERVING:** Calories: 676; Total fat: 26g; Protein: 23g; Sodium: 127mg; Fiber: 21g

# CHANA MASALA

VARIATION ON BASIC BEANS

Chana masala is one of my favorite dishes to order when I visit an Indian restaurant, so I was happy to discover how easy and inexpensive it is to make at home. Try it over steamed rice with a side of veggies. **SERVINGS: 4**

GLUTEN-FREE
SOY-FREE
NUT-FREE
BUDGET-FRIENDLY

4½ cups cooked chickpeas (or 3 cans, drained and rinsed)
1 medium yellow onion, finely diced
1 (14.5-ounce) can diced tomatoes, with juice
1 (1-inch) piece fresh ginger, peeled and minced
1 serrano or jalapeño chile, seeded and minced
1½ teaspoons minced garlic (3 cloves)
2 teaspoons garam masala
2 teaspoons smoked paprika
2 teaspoons ground coriander
1 teaspoon ground cumin
¼ teaspoon ground turmeric
½ teaspoon salt
½ teaspoon freshly ground black pepper
¼ cup water
Handful spinach, chopped (optional)

PREP TIME: 15 MINUTES
COOK TIME: 6 TO 8 HOURS

1. Combine the chickpeas, onion, diced tomatoes, ginger, jalapeño, garlic, garam masala, paprika, coriander, cumin, turmeric, salt, pepper, water, and spinach (if using) in the slow cooker.

2. Cook on low for 6 to 8 hours.

3. Using a potato masher, mash one-third of the chickpeas in the slow cooker before serving.

**PER SERVING:** Calories: 406; Total fat: 7g; Protein: 21g; Sodium: 331mg; Fiber: 20g

# MARINARA SAUCE

I used canned tomatoes in this recipe for convenience, but if you prefer fresh tomatoes, you can use those instead. This is a great recipe to make when tomatoes are in season. You can freeze it in individual servings and have marinara for the year. **SERVINGS: 4**

GLUTEN-FREE
SOY-FREE
NUT-FREE
BUDGET-FRIENDLY

1 (28-ounce) can
   crushed tomatoes
1 (28-ounce) can diced
   tomatoes, with juice
1 (6-ounce) can tomato paste
1 medium onion, diced
2½ teaspoons minced garlic
   (5 cloves)
2 bay leaves
1 tablespoon dried basil
1 tablespoon brown sugar
1 tablespoon balsamic vinegar
1½ teaspoons dried oregano
½ teaspoon red pepper flakes
1 teaspoon salt
½ teaspoon freshly ground
   black pepper

PREP TIME: 15 MINUTES
COOK TIME: 5 HOURS

1. Place the crushed tomatoes, diced tomatoes, tomato paste, onion, garlic, bay leaves, basil, brown sugar, balsamic vinegar, oregano, red pepper flakes, salt, and pepper in the slow cooker, and stir thoroughly.

2. Cover and cook on low for 5 hours.

**INGREDIENT VARIATION:** You'll need about 10 to 12 fresh tomatoes to equal each 28-ounce can.

PER SERVING: Calories: 178; Total fat: <1g; Protein: 9g; Sodium: 1,016mg; Fiber: 12g

# SPAGHETTI-SQUASH
# NOODLES IN MARINARA

VARIATION ON MARINARA SAUCE

Growing up, my palate was pretty limited. I knew what the basic produce options tasted like, but some were completely foreign to me, like spaghetti squash. When I finally tried it a few years ago, I was amazed that a vegetable could satisfy my appetite the same way pasta could. If you're trying to cut back on carbs, this is a good, filling option for dinner. SERVINGS: 4

GLUTEN-FREE
SOY-FREE
NUT-FREE
BUDGET-FRIENDLY

1 (28-ounce) can
    crushed tomatoes
1 (28-ounce) can
    diced tomatoes
1 (6-ounce) can tomato paste
1 medium onion, diced
2½ teaspoons minced garlic
    (5 cloves)
2 bay leaves
1 tablespoon dried basil
1 tablespoon brown sugar
1 tablespoon balsamic vinegar
1½ teaspoons dried oregano
½ teaspoon red pepper flakes
1 teaspoon salt
½ teaspoon freshly ground
    black pepper
1 medium spaghetti squash

PREP TIME: 15 MINUTES
COOK TIME: 5 HOURS

1. Place the crushed tomatoes, diced tomatoes, tomato paste, onion, garlic, bay leaves, basil, brown sugar, balsamic vinegar, oregano, red pepper flakes, salt, and pepper in a slow cooker, and stir thoroughly.

2. Cut the spaghetti squash in half, scoop out the seeds, and place the cut squash halves on top of the tomato mixture in the slow cooker.

3. Cover and cook on low for 5 hours.

4. Remove the spaghetti squash and rake out the insides using a fork until it forms spaghetti-like noodles. Serve with a scoop of marinara sauce.

**LOVE YOUR LEFTOVERS:** This recipe will yield more marinara sauce than you need. Store leftovers in an airtight container in your refrigerator for up to 5 days.

**TIPS FOR TWO:** To get the most out of this meal, serve smaller portions of spaghetti squash and marinara alongside Kale Caesar Salad (page 44). Refrigerate the rest for lunch during the week.

PER SERVING: Calories: 210; Total fat: 1g; Protein: 10g; Sodium: 1,034mg; Fiber: 12g

# STUFFED BELL PEPPERS IN MARINARA SAUCE

VARIATION ON MARINARA SAUCE

The filling in this recipe is very versatile, so don't be afraid to play with it. You can add some corn kernels, mix it up with a Tex-Mex spice blend, or change the type of beans you use. SERVINGS: 4

GLUTEN-FREE
SOY-FREE
NUT-FREE
BUDGET-FRIENDLY

FOR THE MARINARA
1 (28-ounce) can
    crushed tomatoes
1 (28-ounce) can diced
    tomatoes
1 (6-ounce) can tomato paste
1 medium yellow onion, diced
2½ teaspoons minced garlic
    (5 cloves)
2 bay leaves
1 tablespoon dried basil
1 tablespoon brown sugar
1 tablespoon balsamic vinegar
1½ teaspoons dried oregano
½ teaspoon red pepper flakes
1 teaspoon salt
½ teaspoon freshly ground
    black pepper

FOR THE STUFFED PEPPERS
4 medium bell peppers
    (any color)
2 (15-ounce) cans black beans,
    drained and rinsed
½ cup uncooked quinoa, rinsed
2 medium zucchini, chopped

PREP TIME: 15 MINUTES
COOK TIME: 6 HOURS

1. Place the crushed tomatoes, diced tomatoes, tomato paste, onion, garlic, bay leaves, basil, brown sugar, balsamic vinegar, oregano, red pepper flakes, salt, and pepper in a slow cooker, and stir thoroughly. Remove 1½ cups of the mixture and set aside.

2. Slice off the tops of the bell peppers, remove the seeds and scrape them with a spoon to hollow them out. Place the bell peppers cut-side up inside the marinara sauce.

3. In a medium bowl, mix the black beans, quinoa, zucchini, and the reserved 1½ cups of marinara sauce. Divide the filling evenly among the prepared bell peppers.

4. Cover and cook on low for 6 hours.

**LOVE YOUR LEFTOVERS:** Chop the usable parts of the bell pepper tops and add them to your marinara, or throw them in the freezer for when you make a vegetable broth.

**PER SERVING:** Calories: 476; Total fat: 3g; Protein: 25g; Sodium: 1,033mg; Fiber: 23g

# VERY EASY VEGETABLE BROTH

When I'm feeling fancy, I like to make my own broth instead of buying my usual bouillon cubes. Saving vegetable scraps helps reduce my food waste (see tip below), and I like that I can customize the taste by adding more of the vegetable flavors I want to highlight. SERVINGS: 4

NUT-FREE
BUDGET-FRIENDLY

PREP TIME: 15 MINUTES
COOK TIME: 8 HOURS

1½ teaspoons olive oil
1 large yellow onion,
    thinly sliced
4 whole garlic cloves, crushed
2 celery stalks, chopped
3 carrots, scrubbed and sliced
1 medium potato, peeled and
    cut into 1-inch chunks
¼ cup chopped parsley leaves
1½ tablespoons soy sauce
½ teaspoon peppercorns
7 cups water
1 teaspoon salt

1. Drizzle the oil into the bottom of a slow cooker.

2. Add the onion, garlic, celery, carrots, potato, parsley leaves, soy sauce, peppercorns, water, and salt to the slow cooker. Stir to combine, and cook on low for 8 hours.

3. Let the stock cool, then strain it into a bowl using a colander. Press the vegetables to extract all available juices. Store in the refrigerator for up to 5 days, or freeze for up to 3 months.

**COOKING TIP:** For a more flavorful broth, place the onions, garlic, celery, carrots, and potato in a casserole dish, and drizzle with oil, salt, and pepper. Roast for 15 minutes, turn the vegetables, and roast again for 15 minutes, then proceed with the recipe as written.

**LOVE YOUR LEFTOVERS:** This broth is a great way to minimize food waste. Keep a plastic bag in your freezer and toss in onion trimmings and butts of celery and carrots, or any other produce scraps you'd like in your broth.

**PER SERVING:** Calories: 88; Total fat: 2g; Protein: 2g; Sodium: 977mg; Fiber: 3g

# MISO VEGETABLE SOUP

VARIATION ON VERY EASY VEGETABLE BROTH

Napa cabbage originated in China, which is why it's also known as "Chinese cabbage." In Chinese culture, it's a sign of prosperity, and it's a heavily used ingredient in China, Japan, Korea, and many other Asian countries. My Japanese-American grandfather put it in all of his soups, and now I put it in many of mine. **SERVINGS: 4**

NUT-FREE
BUDGET-FRIENDLY

PREP TIME: 15 MINUTES
COOK TIME: 7 TO 8 HOURS

6 cups Very Easy Vegetable
  Broth (page 14) or
  store bought
1 tablespoon white miso paste
½ head napa
  cabbage, chopped
2 carrots, scrubbed and sliced
1 celery stalk, diced
1 teaspoon minced garlic
  (2 cloves)
1 (½-inch) piece fresh ginger,
  peeled and minced
¼ teaspoon red pepper flakes
  (optional)
½ package rice noodles
  (about 4 ounces, optional)

1. Combine the vegetable broth, miso paste, cabbage, carrots, celery, garlic, ginger, and red pepper flakes (if using) in a slow cooker. Stir to combine.

2. Cover and cook for 7 to 8 hours on low or 3 to 4 hours on high.

3. If using the rice noodles, add them to the slow cooker 20 minutes before serving.

**PER SERVING:** Calories: 126; Total fat: 3g; Protein: 9g; Sodium: 1,342mg; Fiber: 2g

# MINESTRONE SOUP

VARIATION ON VERY EASY VEGETABLE BROTH

The best thing about a soup like this is that it lets you clean out your refrigerator and use up any produce that's about to expire. Add your spinach before it goes slimy or your broccoli before it gets rubbery. Or, if you prefer, get a big batch of vegetables fresh from the grocery store—the soup will taste great and be packed with nutrition either way. **SERVINGS: 4**

NUT-FREE
BUDGET-FRIENDLY

PREP TIME: 15 MINUTES
COOK TIME: 6 HOURS

6 cups Very Easy Vegetable
    Broth (page 14) or
    store bought
1 (14.5-ounce) can diced
    tomatoes, with juice
2 carrots, scrubbed, halved,
    and sliced
2 celery stalks, sliced
2 medium Yukon or red
    potatoes, diced
1 cup frozen broccoli or
    green beans
1 medium yellow onion, diced
2 teaspoons minced garlic
    (4 cloves)
2 cups stemmed,
    chopped kale
1 (15-ounce) can red kidney
    beans, drained and rinsed
1 (15-ounce) can black beans,
    drained and rinsed
1 (8-ounce) can tomato sauce
1 teaspoon dried oregano
1 teaspoon ground cumin
2 bay leaves
1 cup small tubular or
    elbow pasta

1. Place the vegetable broth, diced tomatoes, carrots, celery, potatoes, broccoli or green beans, onion, garlic, kale, kidney beans, black beans, tomato sauce, oregano, cumin, and bay leaves in a slow cooker. Mix well.

2. Cover and cook on low for 5 hours, 45 minutes.

3. Turn the slow cooker to high, add the pasta, and continue to cook for 15 minutes more, or until the pasta is tender.

**INGREDIENT TIP:** If you're using russet potatoes, peel them before dicing to avoid a coarse, gritty texture.

**PER SERVING:** Calories: 661; Total fat: 4g; Protein: 40g; Sodium: 1,516mg; Fiber: 24g

# FEEL-BETTER BROTH

People in many cultures have been using ginger and garlic to fight illness for centuries. When you're feeling under the weather, this broth will help boost your immune system, clear your sinuses, and ensure you're getting enough liquids. **SERVINGS: 4**

NUT-FREE
BUDGET-FRIENDLY

PREP TIME: 15 MINUTES
COOK TIME: 8 HOURS

1½ teaspoons olive oil
1 large yellow onion,
    thinly sliced
2 celery stalks, chopped
3 carrots, sliced
1 green bell pepper, chopped
7 whole garlic cloves, smashed
4 (1-inch) pieces fresh ginger,
    peeled and smashed
Juice of ½ lemon
2 tablespoons
    chopped cilantro
1½ tablespoons soy sauce
1 teaspoon salt
½ teaspoon peppercorns
Splash hot sauce (optional)
7 cups water

1.  Drizzle the oil into the bottom of a slow cooker.
2.  Add the onion, celery, carrots, bell pepper, garlic, ginger, lemon juice, cilantro, soy sauce, salt, peppercorns, and hot sauce (if using). Then add the water.
3.  Cover and cook on low for 8 hours.
4.  Let the stock cool, then strain it into a bowl using a colander. Press the vegetables gently to extract all available juices.

**PER SERVING:** Calories: 65; Total fat: 2g; Protein: 1g; Sodium: 637mg; Fiber: 2g

# SICK-DAY SOUP

## VARIATION ON FEEL-BETTER BROTH

This Sick-Day Soup is inspired by a recipe my friend Terrence posted on the blog *Plant Based on a Budget*. His mom used to make it for him when he was sick and then he started making it for his family when they were sick, and now, because of his generosity in sharing this recipe, I make it for my family when they're sick. Hopefully it makes your family feel better, too. **SERVINGS: 4**

NUT-FREE
BUDGET-FRIENDLY

7 cups Feel-Better Broth
(page 17)
1 head cabbage, chopped into
bite-size pieces
1 medium yellow onion, diced
1 red bell pepper, diced
1½ teaspoons minced garlic
(3 cloves)
1 (1-inch) piece fresh ginger,
peeled and minced
1 package extra-firm tofu,
diced and pressed to
remove excess water
1 (6- to 8-ounce) package rice
noodles (optional)

PREP TIME: 15 MINUTES
COOK TIME: 6 TO 8 HOURS

1.  Combine the broth, cabbage, onion, bell pepper, garlic, and ginger in a slow cooker.

2.  Cover and cook for 5½ to 7½ hours on low or 3½ to 5½ hours on high.

3.  Thirty minutes before serving, add the tofu and rice noodles (if using) to the slow cooker.

**PER SERVING:** Calories: 235; Total fat: 5g; Protein: 10g; Sodium: 689mg; Fiber: 9g

# GARLIC-GINGER QUINOA

VARIATION ON FEEL-BETTER BROTH

If you don't have Feel-Better Broth (page 17), feel free to use regular vegetable broth—it works just fine. This recipe pairs well with some baked tofu and veggies, or serve it on its own topped with marinated tofu cubes. **SERVINGS: 4**

NUT-FREE
BUDGET-FRIENDLY

PREP TIME: 10 MINUTES
COOK TIME: 30 MINUTES

1 tablespoon olive oil
1 cup uncooked quinoa, rinsed
2 cups Feel-Better Broth
　　(page 17)
2 tablespoons soy sauce
½ tablespoon peeled and
　　minced fresh ginger
½ teaspoon minced garlic
　　(1 clove)
2 scallions, thinly sliced
Splash hot sauce (optional)

1.　Heat the olive oil in a saucepan over medium heat.

2.　Stir in the quinoa and allow to toast for 2 to 3 minutes, then add the broth, soy sauce, ginger, and garlic.

3.　Increase the heat and bring to a boil. Cover and reduce the heat to low.

4.　Simmer until all the liquid has been absorbed, about 25 minutes.

5.　Fluff the quinoa with a fork. Garnish with the scallions and hot sauce (if using) and serve.

**INGREDIENT TIP:** Consider purchasing a brand of quinoa that's already rinsed, such as Bob's Red Mill.

**PER SERVING:** Calories: 217; Total fat: 7g; Protein: 7g; Sodium: 1,064mg; Fiber: 4g

# POACHED GARLIC

I recently saw a meme that said, "I see recipes for one clove of garlic. One clove of garlic is not enough for any recipe, unless it's a recipe for 'how to cook one clove of garlic,' and even in this case, use two." That's exactly how I feel about garlic. This recipe yields both garlic cloves and delicious garlic-infused oil to flavor your recipes. **SERVINGS: 8**

GLUTEN-FREE
SOY-FREE
NUT-FREE
BUDGET-FRIENDLY

**3 heads garlic, separated into cloves and peeled**
**1 cup canola or other neutral-flavored oil**

PREP TIME: 5 MINUTES
COOK TIME: 2 HOURS, 30 MINUTES

1. Combine the garlic and oil in the slow cooker.
2. Cover and cook on low for 2 hours, 30 minutes.

**LOVE YOUR LEFTOVERS:** Refrigerate the poached garlic in the infused garlic oil in a tightly sealed container for up to 2 weeks. Use the cloves in recipes that call for fresh garlic, and add the oil to your favorite recipes for an extra boost of garlic flavor.

**INGREDIENT VARIATION:** If you'd like to make herb-flavored garlic oil, add 5 or 6 sprigs of your favorite fresh herb, such as rosemary, to the slow cooker with the garlic and oil. Remove the herbs before storing.

**PER SERVING:** Calories: 244; Total fat: 27g; Protein: 0g; Sodium: 0mg; Fiber: 0g

# POACHED GARLIC AND POTATO SOUP

VARIATION ON POACHED GARLIC

If you're looking for a filling, comforting, inexpensive soup, look no further. Even if I shop at the expensive grocery store in my area, I can make a whole batch for less than $6. SERVINGS: 6

GLUTEN-FREE
SOY-FREE
NUT-FREE
BUDGET-FRIENDLY

¾ cup Poached Garlic cloves
    (page 20), minced
4 cups diced potatoes
2 cups frozen broccoli
½ medium yellow onion, diced
6 cups Very Easy Vegetable
    Broth (page 14) or
    store bought
Juice of ½ lemon
½ teaspoon salt
Freshly ground black pepper
Splash hot sauce (optional)

PREP TIME: 10 MINUTES
COOK TIME: 6 TO 8 HOURS

1. Place the garlic, potatoes, broccoli, onion, vegetable broth, lemon juice, and salt in a slow cooker. Season with pepper and hot sauce (if using), and stir well.

2. Cover and cook on low for 6 to 8 hours or on high for 4 to 6 hours.

3. Use an immersion blender (or a traditional blender) to blend about two-thirds of the soup (or to your desired consistency).

**COOKING TIP:** If you're using russet potatoes, peel them. If you're using Yukon or red potatoes, it's fine to leave the skin on.

**TIPS FOR TWO:** Whip up a batch of this budget-friendly soup and pack it in individual portions for lunches all week long.

PER SERVING: Calories: 148; Total fat: 2g; Protein: 9g; Sodium: 783mg; Fiber: 4g

# GOLDEN GARLIC RICE

This rice is tasty as is, but you can also do what you want to make it your own by adding different spices and using different frozen veggies. One of my favorite things to do to dress it up is turn it into fried rice. I let it sit for a day in the refrigerator, then sauté it in some oil with soy sauce, hot sauce, and small cubes of extra-firm tofu. Yum! SERVINGS: 4

GLUTEN-FREE
SOY-FREE
NUT-FREE
BUDGET-FRIENDLY

1½ tablespoons Poached
    Garlic oil (page 20)
1 cup long-grain white rice
¼ small yellow onion,
    finely chopped
3 Poached Garlic
    cloves, chopped
2 cups Very Easy Vegetable
    Broth (page 14) or
    store bought
½ cup frozen mixed veggies
¼ cup sliced shiitake
    mushrooms

PREP TIME: 15 MINUTES
COOK TIME: 25 MINUTES

1. Add the oil, rice, onion, and garlic to a medium sauté pan. Cook over medium heat, stirring frequently, until the onions become translucent and the rice turns a golden brown (about 2 minutes).

2. Add the vegetable broth, frozen vegetables, and mushrooms.

3. Bring to a boil, cover, and lower to a simmer.

4. Allow to simmer for 20 minutes.

**COOKING TIP:** If you use organic rice that's grown in the United States, it isn't necessary to rinse it before cooking. Rinsing does remove extra starch, though, so if you have an extra minute, rinse your rice in cold water before cooking for perfectly fluffy rice.

**PER SERVING:** Calories: 247; Total fat: 6g; Protein: 7g; Sodium: 392mg; Fiber: 1g

# LAZY LENTILS

Archaeological studies show that humans have been eating lentils for up to 13,000 years. You know why? Because lentils are great! They're a healthy source of protein, and they're easy to throw together in all kinds of dishes, from Quick-Fix Lentil Tacos (page 25), to a lentil shepherd's pie, to a tasty Lentil and Black-Bean Chili (page 26). **SERVINGS: 4**

GLUTEN-FREE
SOY-FREE
NUT-FREE
BUDGET-FRIENDLY

1½ cups green, black, or brown lentils, rinsed

4 cups Very Easy Vegetable Broth (page 14) or store bought

1 medium yellow onion, diced

1 teaspoon minced garlic (2 cloves)

1 teaspoon minced jalapeño pepper (optional)

½ teaspoon salt, plus more for seasoning (optional)

Freshly ground black pepper

PREP TIME: 5 MINUTES
COOK TIME: 6 TO 8 HOURS

1. Combine the lentils, vegetable broth, onion, garlic, jalapeño (if using), and salt in a slow cooker; mix well.

2. Cover and cook on low for 6 to 8 hours. Season with salt (if using) and pepper.

**SERVING SUGGESTION:** Want to make the world's easiest salad? Toss 1 cup cooked lentils with ½ cup chopped tomato, ½ a chopped avocado, a light vinaigrette, and some fresh herbs, such as mint or dill.

**PER SERVING:** Calories: 306; Total fat: 2g; Protein: 24g; Sodium: 1,060mg; Fiber: 23g

# QUICK-FIX LENTIL TACOS

VARIATION ON LAZY LENTILS

These tacos are inspired by my friend Terrence's recipe, originally published on the blog *Plant Based on a Budget*. His version is one of my favorites, but it includes more steps and active time than I usually have during the week. My adaptation using slow-cooked lentils makes this a perfect choice for those nights you want a good dinner but are just too busy or tired to cook. SERVINGS: 6

GLUTEN-FREE
SOY-FREE
NUT-FREE
BUDGET-FRIENDLY

1½ teaspoons canola or other neutral-flavored oil
1 cup cooked Lazy Lentils (page 24)
½ cup mushrooms, minced
2 teaspoons chili powder
1 teaspoon garlic powder
1 teaspoon ground cumin
½ teaspoon smoked paprika
½ teaspoon salt
½ teaspoon dried oregano
½ teaspoon red pepper flakes (optional)
1 cup stemmed and thinly sliced kale
6 tortillas, warmed
1 avocado, pitted, peeled, and sliced
Optional toppings: fresh or caramelized onions, vegan sour cream, shredded lettuce, halved cherry tomatoes, microgreens, cashew cream drizzle

PREP TIME: 5 MINUTES
COOK TIME: 3 TO 4 MINUTES
TOTAL TIME: 10 MINUTES

1. Heat the oil in a sauté pan over medium-low heat. Add the lentils, mushrooms, chili powder, garlic powder, cumin, smoked paprika, salt, oregano, red pepper flakes (if using), and kale, and sauté for 3 to 4 minutes. Add 1 tablespoon of water if the filling seems dry.

2. Serve on the warmed tortillas topped with the avocado and any other desired toppings.

**INGREDIENT VARIATION:** Save time by using half of a 1-ounce package of taco seasoning instead of individual spices. If you like it spicier, use the whole package.

**PER SERVING:** Calories: 238; Total fat: 3g; Protein: 14g; Sodium: 217mg; Fiber: 17g

# LENTIL AND BLACK-BEAN CHILI

Grab a blanket, pick a great romantic comedy, and get cozy with this comforting chili. If you want to save some money, instead of using canned beans you can cook dried black beans, kidney beans, and chickpeas together in the same slow cooker using the Basic Beans recipe (page 8). **SERVINGS: 6**

GLUTEN-FREE
SOY-FREE
NUT-FREE
BUDGET-FRIENDLY

1½ cups cooked Lazy Lentils
(page 24)
2 (15-ounce) cans black beans,
drained and rinsed
1 (15-ounce) can red kidney
beans, drained and rinsed
1 (15-ounce) can chickpeas,
drained and rinsed
1 (14.5-ounce) can diced
tomatoes, with juice
1 cup Very Easy Vegetable
Broth (page 14) or
store bought
1 medium yellow onion, diced
1 medium bell pepper, diced
1 jalapeño pepper, minced
2 teaspoons minced garlic
(4 cloves)
3 tablespoons chili powder
2 tablespoons ground cumin
½ teaspoon salt, plus more for
seasoning (optional)

PREP TIME: 15 MINUTES
COOK TIME: 8 HOURS

1. Combine the lentils, black beans, red kidney beans, chickpeas, diced tomatoes, vegetable broth, onion, bell pepper, jalapeño, garlic, chili powder, cumin, and salt in a slow cooker; mix well.

2. Cover and cook on low for 8 hours. Season with more salt (if using).

**INGREDIENT TIP:** Remove the seeds from the jalapeño if you don't like your chili too spicy.

**PER SERVING:** Calories: 716; Total fat: 6g; Protein: 45g; Sodium: 387mg; Fiber: 40g

# BAKED POTATOES FOR BUSY PEOPLE

These potatoes are a filling weekly staple with endless possibilities for toppings. Top with Mushroom Gravy (page 126) or Presto Pesto (page 132) with halved cherry tomatoes, or stick to the basics with some vegan butter and freshly ground black pepper. **SERVINGS: 4**

GLUTEN-FREE
SOY-FREE
NUT-FREE
BUDGET-FRIENDLY

**4 to 6 medium russet or Yukon gold potatoes, peeled and rinsed**
**1½ tablespoons olive oil**
**Pinch salt**

PREP TIME: 10 MINUTES
COOK TIME: 7½ TO 8 HOURS

1. Poke each potato with a fork several times.

2. Rub the potatoes with olive oil and sprinkle with salt.

3. Cover each individual potato tightly with aluminum foil and place in a slow cooker.

4. Cover and cook on low for 7½ to 8 hours or on high for 6 hours.

**WARNING:** Use oven mitts when removing the potatoes. The aluminum foil will be hot.

**COOKING TIP:** If you're using these to make Mashed Potatoes (page 30), use red or Yukon potatoes instead of russet.

**PER SERVING:** Calories: 192; Total fat: 6g; Protein: 4g; Sodium: 52mg; Fiber: 5g

# BAKED-POTATO TACOS

## VARIATION ON BAKED POTATOES FOR BUSY PEOPLE

I don't discriminate when it comes to food—especially tacos. I love me some basic tacos, but these take Taco Tuesday to an entirely different level of goodness by using a potato instead of a tortilla to hold the taco filling. I included my favorite toppings, but feel free to get more creative. Keep it simple, or incorporate Frijoles de la Olla (page 69), Super Simple Salsa (page 128), or Nacho Cheese (page 125). **SERVINGS: 2**

GLUTEN-FREE
SOY-FREE
NUT-FREE
BUDGET-FRIENDLY

**4 Baked Potatoes for Busy People (page 27)**
**1 to 2 cups Lazy Lentils (page 24)**
**1 Roma tomato, diced**
**3 scallions, thinly sliced**
**Pinch salt**
**Freshly ground black pepper**

PREP TIME: 10 MINUTES

1.  When the baked potatoes are cool enough to handle, cut a thin piece off the top of each potato. Using a spoon, scoop the flesh out of each potato to make a bowl, leaving one-quarter of the potato flesh around the edges for support.

2.  Fill each hollowed-out potato with lentils.

3.  Top each potato with tomato, and scallions. Season with salt and pepper.

**INGREDIENT VARIATION:** If you don't have time to make the jackfruit carnitas, or you want more of a protein-packed filling, you can use some pinto beans or another meat alternative like Beyond Meat Beefy Crumble or Ground Beef Style Tofurky Grounds.

**LOVE YOUR LEFTOVERS:** Use the insides you scooped out of the potatoes to make Mashed Potatoes (page 30).

**PER SERVING:** Calories: 433; Total fat: 2g; Protein: 9g; Sodium: 167mg; Fiber: 11g

# MASHED POTATOES

Traditional stove-top mashed potatoes are great, but who has time to peel potatoes, chop them into chunks, wait for them to boil, and then drain them? Not me. This recipe is much more my style. **SERVINGS: 4**

GLUTEN-FREE
SOY-FREE
NUT-FREE
BUDGET-FRIENDLY

6 large red or Yukon potatoes,
    baked (see Baked Potatoes,
    for Busy People page 27)
1 tablespoon vegan butter
Pinch salt
Freshly ground black pepper
½ to 1½ cups unsweetened
    nondairy milk
Sliced scallions, for garnish

PREP TIME: 10 MINUTES

1. When your potatoes are done baking, carefully remove the aluminum foil and return them to the slow cooker. Mash the potatoes with a potato masher. Add the vegan butter, season with salt and pepper, and begin adding the nondairy milk ½ cup at a time, stirring, until the mixture reaches your desired consistency.

2. Keep the slow cooker set to warm until ready to serve.

**INGREDIENT TIP:** Half of the fiber in a potato comes from the skin, so unless you're using russet potatoes, leave the skin on.

**PER SERVING:** Calories: 384; Total fat: 18g; Protein: 7g; Sodium: 100mg; Fiber: 9g

# REALLY EASY ROASTED VEGETABLES

Roasting veggies in your slow cooker is a low-effort way of using whatever produce in your refrigerator is about to expire. I've given you my go-to recipe, but feel free to use whatever veggies you have. **SERVINGS: 4**

GLUTEN-FREE
SOY-FREE
NUT-FREE
BUDGET-FRIENDLY

1 to 2 tablespoons olive oil
2 bell peppers, chopped
2 cups broccoli florets
2 carrots, sliced
3 small zucchini, halved
    lengthwise and cut into
    1-inch chunks
1 small red onion, sliced
½ teaspoon garlic salt

PREP TIME: 10 MINUTES
COOK TIME: 5 TO 6 HOURS

1. Drizzle the olive oil into the bottom of the slow cooker. Add the bell peppers, broccoli florets, carrots, zucchini, red onion, and garlic salt. Mix thoroughly so that the veggies are evenly coated.

2. Cover and cook on low for 5 to 6 hours or on high for 3 to 4 hours. Use a slotted spoon to remove the vegetables from the slow cooker.

**COOKING TIP:** These turn out softer than oven-roasted vegetables. If you want crisp-tender vegetables, cook them for a shorter amount of time.

**LOVE YOUR LEFTOVERS:** Some vegetables produce more liquid than others when cooked in this manner. If you have leftover juice from the roasted veggies, don't toss it out! Instead, add it to a soup for extra flavor and nutrition.

**PER SERVING:** Calories: 143; Total fat: 8g; Protein: 4g; Sodium: 53mg; Fiber: 5g

# PEANUT-SAUCE ROASTED VEGGIES

VARIATION ON REALLY EASY ROASTED VEGGIES

Toss this dish together in a hurry with recipes you've made in advance. Don't love peanut sauce? That's okay. This recipe can be made with many of the sauces in this book, such as Delicious Tahini Dressing (page 135) or Mushroom Gravy (page 126). Try it over rice with sautéed or baked tofu. **SERVINGS: 4**

BUDGET-FRIENDLY

1 batch **Really Easy Roasted Vegetables** (page 31)

1 batch **Perfect Peanut Sauce** (page 134)

**Splash hot sauce or pinch red pepper flakes** (optional)

PREP TIME: 5 MINUTES

In a large bowl, toss the roasted vegetables with the peanut sauce and hot sauce or red pepper flakes (if using).

......................................................................

**PER SERVING:** Calories: 358; Total fat: 27g; Protein: 13g; Sodium: 429mg; Fiber: 7g

# ROASTED VEGETABLE SOUP

This recipe is an easy way to put your roasted veggies to use. You don't have to do any additional cooking besides heating your vegetable broth before pouring it into the slow cooker. Easy peasy and ready to serve! SERVINGS: 4

NUT-FREE
BUDGET-FRIENDLY

1 batch Really Easy Roasted Vegetables (page 31)
6 cups Very Easy Vegetable Broth (page 14) or store bought, heated
½ cup finely chopped fresh herbs, such as parsley, cilantro, or chives
½ teaspoon salt
¼ teaspoon freshly ground black pepper
Splash hot sauce (optional)

PREP TIME: 10 MINUTES

1. Prepare the roasted vegetables according to the recipe. At the end of the cooking time, add the heated broth, herbs, salt, pepper, and hot sauce (if using) to the slow cooker.

2. Set the slow cooker to warm and keep covered until ready to serve.

**INGREDIENT VARIATION:** If you have a batch of Poached Garlic (page 20) on hand, it's a tasty addition to this soup. For a heartier soup, drain and rinse a can of your favorite beans and add them to the broth before heating.

PER SERVING: Calories: 203; Total fat: 10g; Protein: 12g; Sodium: 1,493mg; Fiber: 5g

# CARAMELIZED ONIONS

This recipe makes a huge batch of onions that you can use throughout the week on top of baked tofu or in soups, chili, or stir-fries. You can also freeze it in small, ready-to-use batches. I added sugar to this recipe, but if you're trying to cut down, just leave it out—the onions won't be as sweet, but they'll still be delicious. **SERVINGS: 4**

GLUTEN-FREE
SOY-FREE
NUT-FREE
BUDGET-FRIENDLY

**8 yellow onions, thinly sliced**
**¼ cup canola or other neutral-flavored oil**
**1 teaspoon salt**
**½ teaspoon brown sugar**

PREP TIME: 10 MINUTES
COOK TIME: 10 HOURS

1. Combine the onions, oil, salt, and brown sugar in a slow cooker. Mix thoroughly.

2. Cover and cook on low for 10 hours.

**TIP:** If after 10 hours the onions are too wet for you, drain the liquid and cook with the lid off for another hour or two.

**LOVE YOUR LEFTOVERS:** Make sure to save any excess liquid to add to a soup. Onions make everything more delicious!

**PER SERVING:** Calories: 210; Total fat: 14g; Protein: 2g; Sodium: 590mg; Fiber: 5g

# SHIITAKE MUSHROOM SOUP

Shiitakes are one of the most popular mushrooms in the world and are easily found at most grocery stores. They provide a rich, meaty texture in vegetarian dishes, as well as an abundance of good nutrition. **SERVINGS: 4**

GLUTEN-FREE
SOY-FREE
NUT-FREE
BUDGET-FRIENDLY

2 cups Caramelized Onions
    (page 34)
4 large shiitake mushroom
    caps, sliced
2 teaspoons minced garlic
    (4 cloves)
6 cups Very Easy Vegetable
    Broth (page 14) or
    store bought
½ teaspoon salt
Splash hot sauce or pinch red
    pepper flakes (optional)
Freshly ground black pepper

PREP TIME: 10 MINUTES
COOK TIME: 6 TO 8 HOURS

1. Combine the caramelized onions, mushroom caps, garlic, vegetable broth, salt, and hot sauce or red pepper flakes (if using) in a slow cooker; mix well.

2. Cover and cook on low for 6 to 8 hours. Season with pepper before serving.

**INGREDIENT VARIATION:** For even more flavor, replace the garlic in this recipe with some Poached Garlic (page 20).

**PER SERVING:** Calories: 311; Total fat: 16g; Protein: 11g; Sodium: 2,199mg; Fiber: 6g

# BBQ TOFU WITH CARAMELIZED ONIONS

The classic tang of barbecue sauce is the perfect balance to the rich sweetness of caramelized onions. This dish makes a great meal when served with rice and a small salad, or works perfectly in a barbecue sandwich. SERVINGS: 2

SOY-FREE
NUT-FREE
BUDGET-FRIENDLY

1 tablespoon canola or other neutral-flavored oil
1 package extra-firm tofu, sliced ½-inch thick and pressed to remove excess water
½ cup prepared barbecue sauce
Cooked rice, for serving (optional)
1 cup Caramelized Onions (page 34)

PREP TIME: 5 MINUTES
COOK TIME: 10 MINUTES

1. Preheat a skillet over medium-high heat.

2. Add the oil to the skillet, then carefully add the tofu in a single layer. Fry for about 5 minutes. Flip each piece of tofu and fry for another 5 minutes.

3. Add the barbecue sauce to the skillet. Turn the tofu slices to coat evenly. Spoon over the rice (if using) and top with the caramelized onions.

**INGREDIENT TIP:** I buy vacuum-sealed tofu instead of the water-packed type, and I find that it has less water to press. If you're new to tofu, don't be intimidated. Simply wrap each slice of tofu in a paper towel and press gently to remove excess water.

**TIPS FOR TWO:** If you're serving this with rice, a side of veggies, or a salad, you'll have enough tofu for at least one lunch sandwich. To make a BBQ tofu sandwich, pile cold tofu and caramelized onions on a bun with thinly sliced raw veggies and some vegan ranch dressing.

**PER SERVING:** Calories: 225; Total fat: 13g; Protein: 6g; Sodium: 652mg; Fiber: 3g

# FRUIT COMPOTE

Fruit compote is a tasty topping that makes me feel healthy when I want a little extra something with my vegan vanilla ice cream. It's technically a proper serving of produce, right? If you don't feel like ice cream, compote is also great on breakfast oats, on toast, with a savory tofu entrée, and more. SERVINGS: 6

GLUTEN-FREE
SOY-FREE
NUT-FREE
BUDGET-FRIENDLY

1 (16-ounce) package frozen berries or peaches
1 cup apple juice
1 cup dried cranberries
2 medium tart apples, such as Granny Smith, peeled, cored and sliced
¼ cup brown sugar
1 cinnamon stick
1 tablespoon orange zest
Juice of ½ orange

PREP TIME: 10 MINUTES
COOK TIME: 8 HOURS

1. Combine the frozen fruit, apple juice, dried cranberries, apples, brown sugar, cinnamon stick, orange zest, and orange juice in a slow cooker.
2. Cover and cook on low for 8 hours.
3. Remove the cinnamon stick and serve warm.

**INGREDIENT TIP:** Depending on your preferred level of sweetness, you can make this compote with sweetened or unsweetened dried cranberries.

**PER SERVING:** Calories: 122; Total fat: <1g; Protein: <1g; Sodium: 5mg; Fiber: 4g

# BREAKFAST QUINOA TOPPED WITH FRUIT COMPOTE

VARIATION ON FRUIT COMPOTE

Quinoa is one of many ingredients I didn't try until I was an adult. I was under the impression that it was fancy and expensive, but it's actually a basic staple that you can usually purchase for less in the bulk-bin section. A seed from a South American plant, quinoa is high in protein and is considered a super-food. **SERVINGS: 6**

GLUTEN-FREE
SOY-FREE
NUT-FREE
BUDGET-FRIENDLY

1 cup uncooked quinoa, rinsed

2 cups water

1 cup canned full-fat coconut milk

2 tablespoons maple syrup or agave nectar

1 teaspoon vanilla extract

1 teaspoon ground cinnamon

¼ teaspoon salt

Fruit Compote (page 37), for serving

Optional toppings: nuts, seeds, sliced bananas, dried fruit

PREP TIME: 10 MINUTES
COOK TIME: 7 TO 8 HOURS

1. Place the quinoa, water, coconut milk, maple syrup, vanilla extract, cinnamon, and salt into the slow cooker. Mix well.

2. Cover and cook on low for 7 to 8 hours.

3. Spoon into bowls and top each serving with ½ cup of fruit compote and toppings (if using).

**INGREDIENT VARIATION:** If you want to mix it up, treat this dish as you would oatmeal. You can include dried fruit, top with fresh fruit, or add nuts or seeds.

**LOVE YOUR LEFTOVERS:** Before you measure out the coconut milk, give the can a good shake to distribute the cream that rises to the top. Freeze leftover coconut milk in ice-cube trays to add to smoothies, rice dishes, or soups.

PER SERVING: Calories: 339; Total fat: 12g; Protein: 6g; Sodium: 112mg; Fiber: 8g

# APPLE-PIE OATMEAL

VARIATION ON FRUIT COMPOTE

Throw your ingredients in the slow cooker before you go to sleep, and wake up to a home filled with the most comforting and delicious aromas. The best part? All the cooking is done while you're asleep, so all you need to do is wake up and eat! **SERVINGS: 6**

GLUTEN-FREE
SOY-FREE
NUT-FREE
BUDGET-FRIENDLY

1 cup steel-cut oats
3 cups nondairy milk, plus
    more for serving (optional)
½ cup apple juice or water
1 medium apple, peeled, cored
    and finely diced
½ cup raisins
2 tablespoons brown sugar
2 teaspoons ground cinnamon
1 teaspoon vanilla extract
3 cups Fruit Compote
    (page 37), for serving
Optional toppings: chopped
    nuts or seeds, chopped
    apples, dried fruit, granola

PREP TIME: 10 MINUTES
COOK TIME: 5 TO 8 HOURS

1. Place the oats, nondairy milk, apple juice, apple, raisins, brown sugar, cinnamon, and vanilla extract in the slow cooker.

2. Cover and cook on low for 5 to 8 hours, depending on your preferred texture—firmer to softer oats.

3. Spoon into bowls and top each serving with ½ cup of fruit compote, plus your choice of additional toppings and a splash of nondairy milk (if using).

**INGREDIENT TIP:** If you want the apples to be very soft, sauté them in a pan for a few minutes with a drop of oil before adding them to the slow cooker. If your oats seem too runny, cook them for an additional 30 minutes with the lid off.

**PER SERVING:** Calories: 530; Total fat: 30g; Protein: 6g; Sodium: 27mg; Fiber: 10g

Spicy Tomato-Lentil Stew (page 43)

# MAIN DISHES

# SPICY TOMATO-LENTIL STEW

This lentil stew is something that's easy to toss together using pantry ingredients, and it freezes beautifully. The spicy flavors are cooled down when you pair it with Kale Caesar Salad (page 44). It's flexible, too—mix it up by adding any veggies you have in the fridge, like broccoli, cauliflower, or green beans. SERVINGS: 4

GLUTEN-FREE
SOY-FREE
NUT-FREE
BUDGET-FRIENDLY

2 cups dry brown or
    green lentils, rinsed
5 cups water
1 (14.5-ounce) can
    crushed tomatoes
1 (14.5-ounce) can diced
    tomatoes, with juice
2 cups peeled, chopped
    russet potatoes
1 medium yellow onion, diced
½ cup scrubbed
    chopped carrot
½ cup chopped celery
2 tablespoons your favorite
    hot sauce
2 teaspoons minced garlic
    (4 cloves)
2 teaspoons ground cumin
1 teaspoon chili powder
½ teaspoon ground coriander
¼ teaspoon smoked paprika
1 bay leaf
Pinch cayenne pepper
4 vegetable bouillon cubes

PREP TIME: 15 MINUTES
COOK TIME: 6 TO 8 HOURS

1. Combine the lentils, water, crushed tomatoes, diced tomatoes, potatoes, onion, carrot, celery, hot sauce, garlic, cumin, chili powder, coriander, paprika, bay leaf, cayenne pepper, and bouillon cubes in a slow cooker; mix well.

2. Cover and cook on low for 6 to 8 hours.

3. Remove the bay leaf, and serve.

**INGREDIENT VARIATION:** If you don't have bouillon cubes, you can use vegetable broth in place of water.

PER SERVING: Calories: 517; Total fat: 2g; Protein: 32g; Sodium: 1,063mg; Fiber: 38g

# KALE CAESAR SALAD

SERVE WITH SPICY TOMATO-LENTIL STEW

This kale Caesar salad is the brainchild of my dearest friend, Grace. Grace lived at Animal Place Sanctuary, where I worked, and she would regularly make this for us to enjoy during our lunch breaks. It's definitely best when served with plenty of croutons! **SERVINGS: 4**

SOY-FREE
NUT-FREE
BUDGET-FRIENDLY

**FOR THE DRESSING**
½ cup firm tofu
½ cup olive oil
1 teaspoon minced garlic
    (2 cloves)
2½ tablespoons freshly
    squeezed lemon juice
2 tablespoons white vinegar
2 tablespoons Dijon mustard
3½ teaspoons capers
Pinch salt
Freshly ground black pepper

**FOR THE SALAD**
1½ to 2 bunches of curly kale,
    stemmed and torn into
    bite-size pieces
Croutons (optional)

PREP TIME: 10 MINUTES

**TO MAKE THE DRESSING**

1. Add the tofu, oil, garlic, lemon juice, vinegar, and Dijon mustard to a blender. Blend well.

2. Add the capers and mix well. Season with salt and pepper.

**TO MAKE THE SALAD**

1. Place the kale in a large bowl, and thoroughly massage the dressing into the kale.

2. Top with croutons (if using).

**INGREDIENT TIP:** Massaging the kale helps reduce bitterness. Use clean hands to roughly massage it with the dressing for a good 3 to 5 minutes. The kale will turn a brighter green, and it will become softer, chewier, and easier to digest.

**TIPS FOR TWO:** This salad will keep overnight in the fridge if you store the croutons separately. To make a second meal out of it, try adding marinated extra-firm tofu.

**PER SERVING:** Calories: 378; Total fat: 27g; Protein: 5g; Sodium: 220mg; Fiber: <1g

# SPICY ETHIOPIAN LENTIL STEW

Turn up the flavor on your basic lentil stew and enjoy the exotic fragrances and savory tastes of fenugreek, cardamom, chiles, and cinnamon. Ethiopian stews are traditionally served with *injera*, a flatbread made from fermented teff that's used as both accompaniment and utensil. Pita or naan would work just as well. **SERVINGS: 4**

GLUTEN-FREE
SOY-FREE
NUT-FREE
BUDGET-FRIENDLY

1 cup dry red lentils, rinsed
4 cups water
2 cups peeled chopped russet potatoes
1 medium red onion, diced
½ cup chopped carrot
½ cup chopped celery
2 teaspoons minced garlic (4 cloves)
4 vegetable bouillon cubes
2 to 3 tablespoons your favorite hot sauce
1½ tablespoons berbere spice mix
1 tablespoon tomato paste
½ tablespoon ground ginger
1 teaspoon smoked paprika
1 teaspoon ground cumin

PREP TIME: 15 MINUTES
COOK TIME: 6 TO 8 HOURS

1. Combine the lentils, water, potatoes, red onion, carrot, celery, garlic, bouillon cubes, hot sauce, berbere, tomato paste, ginger, smoked paprika, and cumin in a slow cooker; mix well.

2. Cover and cook on low for 6 to 8 hours.

**INGREDIENT VARIATION:** Berbere is a fragrant spice mix used to flavor Ethiopian dishes. If your market doesn't carry it, you can mix your own. Just combine 4½ teaspoons sweet paprika, 2 tablespoons cayenne pepper, 1 teaspoon ground coriander, ½ tablespoon salt, ½ teaspoon ground ginger, ⅛ teaspoon ground cloves, ¼ teaspoon ground cardamom, ¼ teaspoon ground fenugreek, ¼ teaspoon ground nutmeg, and ¼ teaspoon ground allspice.

**PER SERVING:** Calories: 298; Total fat: 1g; Protein: 16g; Sodium: 1,409mg; Fiber: 19g

# RED TOFU CURRY

This simple curry is comforting and gently spiced. The sweet, mild flavors of this dish with its creamy coconut milk sauce make it a great "beginner's curry." If you're not sure you love curry, give this one a try. Serve it with Larb Salad (page 48) for an unforgettable meal. SERVINGS: 4

GLUTEN-FREE
NUT-FREE
BUDGET-FRIENDLY

1 tablespoon canola oil
1 (12-ounce) package
    extra-firm tofu, cut into
    ½-inch cubes and pressed
    to reduce excess water
3 cups baby carrots,
    halved lengthwise
2 cups peeled red or Yukon
    potatoes, chopped into
    bite-size pieces
2 medium yellow
    onions, diced
3 teaspoons minced garlic
    (6 cloves)
1 (1-inch) piece fresh ginger,
    peeled and minced
1¾ cups water
1 cup canned unsweetened
    coconut milk
1½ tablespoons red
    curry paste
1 vegetable bouillon cube
½ teaspoon salt
Cooked rice, for serving
Fresh cilantro, for garnish

PREP TIME: 15 MINUTES
COOK TIME: 6 TO 8 HOURS

1.  In a skillet over medium-high heat, heat the oil. Add the tofu and brown until the edges are crisp, about 5 minutes.

2.  Combine the tofu, baby carrots, potatoes, onions, garlic, ginger, water, coconut milk, red curry paste, bouillon cube, and salt in a slow cooker; mix well.

3.  Cover and cook on low for 6 to 8 hours or on high for 3 to 4 hours.

4.  Serve over rice and garnished with cilantro.

**INGREDIENT VARIATION:** Using baby carrots cuts down on prep time, but if you don't have them, just use peeled, chopped regular carrots.

**PER SERVING:** Calories: 479; Total fat: 20g; Protein: 17g; Sodium: 540mg; Fiber: 10g

# LARB SALAD

In Sacramento, there is a decently sized Hmong community, and I have early childhood memories of eating this traditional Lao dish with my friends at school. It's traditionally made with meat and can also be made with mushrooms, but I chose to use an extra-firm tofu base. SERVINGS: 4

NUT-FREE
BUDGET-FRIENDLY

PREP TIME: 5 MINUTES
COOK TIME: 4 TO 5 MINUTES

1 teaspoon oil
1 package extra-firm tofu, pressed to remove excess water and crumbled
Juice of 2 limes, divided
¼ cup thinly sliced shallots
1 scallion, thinly sliced
5 cilantro sprigs, sliced
2 tablespoons soy sauce
1 or 2 mint sprigs, chopped
¾ teaspoon ground dried Thai chiles (or red pepper flakes)
8 lettuce leaves (iceberg or romaine), for serving

1. Heat the oil in a medium sauté pan over medium heat. Add the tofu and the juice of ½ lime, and sauté for 4 to 5 minutes, until the tofu is light brown.

2. Place the tofu in a bowl and add the shallots, scallion, cilantro, soy sauce, mint, chiles, and the juice of the 1½ remaining limes. Mix well.

3. Spoon onto lettuce leaves and serve.

**INGREDIENT VARIATION:** If you like spicier foods, try adding a minced jalapeño or serrano chile, including its seeds.

**TIPS FOR TWO:** Larb salad stores well in the refrigerator. Enjoy half with your curry, then pack the rest into a container for a portable lunch. Wrap the lettuce separately to keep it fresh and crunchy.

PER SERVING: Calories: 96: Total fat: 5g; Protein: 8g; Sodium: 465mg; Fiber: 2g

# QUINOA CURRY

VARIATION ON RED TOFU CURRY

Once you've mastered the basic Red Tofu Curry (page 46), change it up with this variation, which swaps the tofu for quinoa and chickpeas. Quinoa adds a protein boost and a texture similar to ground meat, making it a fantastic way to improve both flavor and texture in hearty soups, stews, and curries. SERVINGS: 4

GLUTEN-FREE
SOY-FREE
NUT-FREE
BUDGET-FRIENDLY

3 cups baby carrots,
    halved lengthwise
2 cups frozen diced
    sweet potato
2 medium yellow
    onions, diced
1 (15-ounce) can chickpeas,
    drained and rinsed
3 teaspoons minced garlic
    (6 cloves)
1 (1-inch) piece fresh ginger,
    peeled and minced
1¾ cups water
1 cup canned unsweetened
    coconut milk
1½ tablespoons yellow
    curry powder
1 vegetable bouillon cube
½ teaspoon salt
½ cup uncooked
    quinoa, rinsed

PREP TIME: 15 MINUTES
COOK TIME: 6 TO 8 HOURS

1. Add the carrots, sweet potato, onions, chickpeas, garlic, ginger, water, coconut milk, curry powder, bouillon cube, and salt to a slow cooker; mix well.

2. Cover and cook on low for 5½ to 7½ hours or on high for 2½ to 3½ hours.

3. Thirty minutes before serving, add the quinoa. Cover and cook.

PER SERVING: Calories: 564; Total fat: 19g; Protein: 18g; Sodium: 566mg; Fiber: 19g

# MIXED-BEAN CHILI

This is the easiest, laziest, tastiest chili in the world. You can clean out your refrigerator by adding any produce that's about to expire. Use the following as a master recipe, then mix it up any way you like, or try the Sweet Potato Chili variation on page 52. SERVINGS: 4

GLUTEN-FREE
SOY-FREE
NUT-FREE
BUDGET-FRIENDLY

5 (15-ounce) cans your choice
   beans, drained and rinsed
1 (15-ounce) can diced
   tomatoes, with juice
1 (6-ounce) can tomato paste
1 cup water
1 green bell pepper, diced
2 cups stemmed and
   chopped kale
½ medium yellow onion, diced
2 tablespoons ground cumin
1 tablespoon chili powder
1 teaspoon minced garlic
   (2 cloves)
1 teaspoon cayenne pepper
Pinch salt

PREP TIME: 15 MINUTES
COOK TIME: 6 TO 7 HOURS

1. Place the beans, diced tomatoes, tomato paste, water, bell pepper, kale, onion, cumin, chili powder, garlic, and cayenne pepper in a slow cooker.

2. Cover and cook on low for 6 to 7 hours.

3. Season with salt and serve.

**LOVE YOUR LEFTOVERS:** Have leftover broccoli stems in the fridge? Don't throw them out. Instead, shave them using a potato peeler and throw them in this recipe. They'll soften, and you won't even know they're there.

**INGREDIENT TIP:** Use a mixture of your favorite beans for this chili, such as pinto, red kidney, black, or cannellini.

PER SERVING: Calories: 823: Total fat: 4g; Protein: 53g; Sodium: 153mg; Fiber: 38g

# TOMATO-AVOCADO SALAD

This salad is simple, fast, and fresh. The cilantro and cumin flavors make for a great accompaniment to any of the chili recipes in this book. Choose perfectly ripe avocados; an avocado that's ready to be used will have dark skin and will yield slightly when gently pressed with your thumb. **SERVINGS: 4**

GLUTEN-FREE
SOY-FREE
NUT-FREE
BUDGET-FRIENDLY

**2 medium vine-ripe tomatoes, chopped**
**1 avocado, pitted, peeled, and chopped**
**¼ cup diced red onion**
**1 tablespoon olive oil**
**1 tablespoon balsamic vinegar**
**1½ teaspoons minced cilantro**
**1 teaspoon freshly squeezed lemon juice**
**½ teaspoon ground cumin**
**Pinch salt**
**Freshly ground black pepper**

PREP TIME: 5 MINUTES

1. Gently combine the tomatoes, avocado, red onion, olive oil, balsamic vinegar, cilantro, lemon juice, and cumin in a bowl.

2. Season with salt and pepper.

**LOVE YOUR LEFTOVERS:** If you're lucky enough to have leftovers (or you decide to double the recipe), try a festive spin on traditional avocado toast. Serve this salad atop toast for a healthy snack.

PER SERVING: Calories: 149: Total fat: 14g; Protein: 2g; Sodium: 46mg; Fiber: 4g

# SWEET POTATO CHILI

VARIATION ON MIXED-BEAN CHILI

This chili is hearty and healthy, with plenty of vitamins, minerals, and fiber. Sweet potatoes provide an earthy sweetness that complements the heat of the cayenne pepper perfectly. Try it with your favorite tortilla chips and a dollop of vegan sour cream. **SERVINGS: 4**

GLUTEN-FREE
SOY-FREE
NUT-FREE
BUDGET-FRIENDLY

2 medium sweet potatoes,
    peeled and cut into
    1-inch cubes
3 (15-ounce) cans your choice
    beans, drained and rinsed
1 (15-ounce) can diced
    tomatoes, with juice
1 (6-ounce) can tomato paste
2 cups stemmed and
    chopped kale
½ yellow onion, diced
2 tablespoons ground cumin
1 tablespoon chili powder
1 teaspoon minced garlic
    (2 cloves)
1 teaspoon cayenne pepper
¼ teaspoon ground cinnamon
1 cup water
Pinch salt

PREP TIME: 15 MINUTES
COOK TIME: 5 TO 6 HOURS

1. Place the sweet potatoes, beans, diced tomatoes, tomato paste, kale, onion, cumin, chili powder, garlic, cayenne pepper, cinnamon, and water in a slow cooker.

2. Cover and cook on low for 5 to 6 hours. Season with salt.

**TIPS FOR TWO:** Serve this chili over brown rice to make it last several meals.

**INGREDIENT VARIATION:** Use 3 cups frozen, precut sweet potatoes or butternut squash in this recipe instead of fresh sweet potatoes.

......................................................................

**PER SERVING:** Calories: 752: Total fat: 3g; Protein: 39g; Sodium: 157mg; Fiber: 33g

# BUTTERNUT SQUASH SOUP

Using frozen, precut butternut squash means almost no prep time, making this the perfect recipe to throw in the slow cooker on a busy morning. Vegan cream cheese stands in for cream in this recipe, for a healthy indulgence you'll love. Adding a simple mixed green salad on the side makes for a perfect light lunch or supper. SERVINGS: 4

GLUTEN-FREE
SOY-FREE
NUT-FREE
BUDGET-FRIENDLY

2 (10-ounce) packages frozen butternut squash

6 cups water

1 medium yellow onion, chopped

1 teaspoon minced garlic (2 cloves)

5 vegetable bouillon cubes

2 bay leaves

¼ teaspoon freshly ground black pepper

⅛ teaspoon cayenne pepper

1 (8-ounce) package vegan cream cheese, cut into chunks

PREP TIME: 15 MINUTES
COOK TIME: 6½ TO 8½ HOURS

1. Combine the butternut squash, water, onion, garlic, bouillon cubes, bay leaves, black pepper, and cayenne pepper in a slow cooker. Stir to mix.

2. Cover and cook on low for 6 to 8 hours.

3. Remove the bay leaves.

4. Using an immersion blender (or a regular blender, working in batches), purée half of the soup.

5. Stir in the cream cheese. Cover and cook on low for 30 minutes longer.

**INGREDIENT VARIATION:** If you'd like to use fresh butternut squash instead of frozen, peel and dice one medium squash.

PER SERVING: Calories: 238: Total fat: 16g; Protein: 4g; Sodium: 999mg; Fiber: 3g

# MIXED GREENS WITH CITRUS DRESSING

SERVE WITH BUTTERNUT SQUASH SOUP

When I first created this recipe, it had all kinds of complicated ingredients like frisée and radicchio, but then I realized that sometimes simpler is better. If you're feeling fancy, feel free to add a handful of each, and maybe some thinly sliced fennel. Yum! SERVINGS: 4

GLUTEN-FREE
SOY-FREE
NUT-FREE
BUDGET-FRIENDLY

**FOR THE DRESSING**
3 tablespoons freshly squeezed orange juice
1½ tablespoons freshly squeezed lime juice
1½ tablespoons extra-virgin olive oil
2 teaspoons agave nectar
1 teaspoon Dijon mustard
1 teaspoon apple cider vinegar
¼ teaspoon salt
⅛ teaspoon freshly ground black pepper

**FOR THE SALAD**
1 (5-ounce) bag mixed baby greens
1 orange, peeled and cut into segments
¾ cup pumpkin seeds

PREP TIME: 10 MINUTES

**TO MAKE THE DRESSING**
In a small bowl, whisk together the orange juice, lime juice, olive oil, agave nectar, Dijon mustard, apple-cider vinegar, salt, and pepper.

**TO MAKE THE SALAD**
1. In a salad bowl, combine the greens, orange segments, and pumpkin seeds.
2. Drizzle the dressing on top and toss gently.

**COOKING TIP:** To segment an orange, cut off the very top and bottom, then use a sharp paring knife to cut away the peel and the white pith, which is bitter and stringy. Use the knife to cut between the membranes to release each individual segment. If this sounds too time-consuming, you can find segmented orange slices packed in juice in the refrigerated section of your market's produce department.

PER SERVING: Calories: 230: Total fat: 17g; Protein: 7g; Sodium: 169mg; Fiber: 2g

# GINGER CURRIED BUTTERNUT SQUASH SOUP

VARIATION ON BUTTERNUT SQUASH SOUP

If you keep a few packages of butternut squash in your freezer, you'll always be ready to make this easy, slightly spicy soup that's perfect if you're feeling under the weather. If you love ginger, double the amount for a spicy, delicious kick. SERVINGS: 4

GLUTEN-FREE
SOY-FREE
NUT-FREE
BUDGET-FRIENDLY

2 (10-ounce) packages frozen butternut squash
6 cups water
1 medium onion, chopped
2 teaspoons curry powder
1 teaspoon minced garlic (2 cloves)
1 (½-inch) piece fresh ginger, peeled and minced
5 vegetable bouillon cubes
¼ teaspoon freshly ground black pepper
⅛ teaspoon cayenne pepper
1 (8-ounce) package vegan cream cheese, cut into chunks

PREP TIME: 15 MINUTES
COOK TIME: 6½ TO 8½ HOURS

1. Combine the butternut squash, water, onion, curry powder, garlic, ginger, bouillon cubes, black pepper, and cayenne pepper in a slow cooker.

2. Cover and cook on low for 6 to 8 hours.

3. Using an immersion blender (or a regular blender, working in batches), blend half of the soup.

4. Stir in the cream cheese. Cover and cook on low for 30 minutes longer.

TIPS FOR TWO: To turn this soup into a hearty meal, pair it with a protein-rich salad, such as Quinoa-and-Bean Salad (page 9), and toasted whole-grain bread.

LOVE YOUR LEFTOVERS: Freeze soups in individual portions, and lunch will never be boring again.

PER SERVING: Calories: 320: Total fat: 21g; Protein: 8g; Sodium: 1,070mg; Fiber: 9g

# SPLIT-PEA SOUP

Split-pea soup is a classic American comfort food—and a great source of protein. Add the Grilled Romaine Hearts with Miso Dressing on page 57, and you have a delicious feast. Making this soup in the slow cooker yields a silky texture every time. Serve it garnished with your favorite croutons for a real treat! **SERVINGS: 4**

GLUTEN-FREE
SOY-FREE
NUT-FREE
BUDGET-FRIENDLY

1 pound dried green split
    peas, rinsed
6 cups water
3 carrots, diced
3 celery stalks, diced
1 medium russet potato,
    peeled and diced
1 small yellow onion, diced
1½ teaspoons minced garlic
    (3 cloves)
5 vegetable bouillon cubes
1 bay leaf
Freshly ground black pepper

PREP TIME: 15 MINUTES
COOK TIME: 6 TO 8 HOURS

1. Combine the split peas, water, carrots, celery, potato, onion, garlic, bouillon cubes, and bay leaf in a slow cooker; mix well.
2. Cover and cook on low for 6 to 8 hours.
3. Remove the bay leaf and season with pepper.

**WARNING:** Be sure to rinse your split peas thoroughly before adding them to the slow cooker. While you're rinsing, sift your fingers through them and look out for small pebbles, which can sometimes find their way into bags of dried split peas and beans.

**INGREDIENT TIP:** If you taste your soup and feel like it's missing something, try adding a few drops of freshly squeezed lemon juice. That little bit of acid will bring out all the other flavors.

**PER SERVING:** Calories: 465: Total fat: 2g; Protein: 30g; Sodium: 838mg; Fiber: 32g

# GRILLED ROMAINE HEARTS WITH MISO DRESSING

SERVE WITH SPLIT-PEA SOUP

Grilling romaine creates a smoky sweetness that is the perfect foil for the salty, umami flavors of miso and sesame in the dressing. Serve this to someone you want to impress! **SERVINGS: 4**

GLUTEN-FREE
SOY-FREE
NUT-FREE
BUDGET-FRIENDLY

**FOR THE DRESSING**

2 tablespoons toasted
    sesame oil
2 tablespoons extra-virgin
    olive oil
1 tablespoon miso paste
1 tablespoon rice vinegar
1 tablespoon freshly squeezed
    lime juice
½ teaspoon grated
    fresh ginger
½ teaspoon minced garlic
    (1 clove)
Pinch red pepper flakes

**FOR THE SALAD**

2 heads romaine lettuce, cut
    lengthwise into quarters
2 tablespoons extra-virgin
    olive oil
Pinch salt
Freshly ground black pepper

PREP TIME: 10 MINUTES
COOK TIME: 5 MINUTES

**TO MAKE THE DRESSING**
Whisk together the sesame oil, olive oil, miso, rice vinegar, lime juice, ginger, garlic and red pepper flakes in a small bowl until well combined. Set aside.

**TO MAKE THE SALAD**

1. Drizzle the lettuce with the olive oil. Add the salt, and season with pepper. Place the lettuce cut-side down on a preheated grill or grill pan. Cook until the lettuce is slightly charred, about 5 minutes.

2. Transfer the lettuce to plates, drizzle with miso dressing, and serve.

**TIPS FOR TWO:** Double the dressing recipe, and serve it over rice, chopped raw veggies, and some diced avocado for a quick vegan sushi bowl.

PER SERVING: Calories: 216: Total fat: 21g; Protein: 1g; Sodium: 209mg; Fiber: 1g

# MISO SPLIT-PEA SOUP

VARIATION ON SPLIT-PEA SOUP

Adding a touch of miso to basic split-pea soup adds tremendous depth of flavor. Miso is an umami flavor that adds the smoky, earthy saltiness that makes a good split-pea soup so satisfying. Try adding a garnish of toasted pumpkin seeds, hemp seeds, or toasted almonds to make this simple soup feel a little fancy. SERVINGS: 4

NUT-FREE
BUDGET-FRIENDLY

PREP TIME: 15 MINUTES
COOK TIME: 6 TO 8 HOURS

1 pound dried green split
    peas, rinsed

3 carrots, diced

3 celery stalks, diced

1 medium potato, peeled
    and diced

1 small yellow onion, diced

3 tablespoons white
    miso paste

1½ teaspoons minced garlic
    (3 cloves)

5 vegetable bouillon cubes

1 bay leaf

6 cups water

1. Combine the split peas, carrots, celery, potato, onion, miso paste, garlic, bouillon cubes, bay leaf, and water in a slow cooker; mix well.

2. Cover and cook on low for 6 to 8 hours.

3. Remove the bay leaf before serving.

**INGREDIENT TIP:** Miso is a fermented paste that's commonly made from soy, grains, and salt. It will last for months in the fridge if the container is properly sealed. It's fairly easy to find gluten-free miso made with buckwheat, rice, or millet. Soy-free miso, made with chickpeas or adzuki beans, can be more difficult to locate, but it's an ingredient worth seeking out if you don't eat soy. Miso is a great ingredient to keep on hand—use it when you want to boost the saltiness and flavor in a soup or stew. If you buy prepared miso soup, look for one that doesn't contain *dashi* (broth made with dried flakes of bonito fish) to ensure it's vegan.

PER SERVING: Calories: 493; Total fat: 3g; Protein: 32g; Sodium: 1,472mg; Fiber: 33g

# TOMATO BISQUE

Yes, you really can make a luscious tomato bisque without using dairy! Cashews and white beans provide the right amount of body and creaminess, making it a perfect choice for a cold day. A peppery arugula salad provides the perfect sharp counterpoint to make this a meal. **SERVINGS: 4**

GLUTEN-FREE
SOY-FREE
BUDGET-FRIENDLY

2 (28-ounce) cans crushed tomatoes

1 (28-ounce) can whole peeled tomatoes, with juice

1 (15-ounce) can white beans, drained and rinsed

½ cup cashew pieces

2 vegetable bouillon cubes

1 tablespoon dried basil

2 teaspoons minced garlic (4 cloves)

3 cups water

Pinch salt

Freshly ground black pepper

PREP TIME: 15 MINUTES
COOK TIME: 6 TO 8 HOURS

1. Combine the crushed tomatoes, whole peeled tomatoes, white beans, cashew pieces, bouillon cubes, dried basil, garlic, and water in a slow cooker.

2. Cover and cook on low for 6 to 8 hours.

3. Using an immersion blender (or a regular blender, working in batches), blend the soup until smooth. Season with salt and pepper.

**INGREDIENT TIP:** The sweetness and flavor of canned tomatoes varies by brand. If your finished soup tastes a little sour, try adding a drop or two of agave nectar or a pinch of cane sugar.

**TIPS FOR TWO:** This tomato soup pairs just as well with a grilled cheese sandwich as it does with a salad. Toast up sandwiches made from your favorite bread and vegan cheese, plus a smear of Presto Pesto (page 132) or prepared chipotle mayo.

**PER SERVING:** Calories: 491; Total fat: 9g; Protein: 28g; Sodium: 1,134mg; Fiber: 24g

# BABY ARUGULA WITH PESTO VINAIGRETTE

SERVE WITH TOMATO BISQUE

The slightly bitter flavor of arugula is accented with creamy avocado and nutty chickpeas for a protein-rich salad that satisfies like a meal. Pesto pairs nicely with either of the tomato soups in this chapter. **SERVINGS: 4**

GLUTEN-FREE
SOY-FREE
BUDGET-FRIENDLY

**FOR THE DRESSING**
2½ tablespoons Presto Pesto
   (page 132)
3 teaspoons olive oil
1½ teaspoons balsamic vinegar
Pinch salt
Freshly ground black pepper

**FOR THE SALAD**
1 (5-ounce) package
   baby arugula
1 medium avocado, pitted,
   peeled, and cubed
1 (15-ounce) can chickpeas,
   drained and rinsed

PREP TIME: 10 MINUTES

**TO MAKE THE DRESSING**
1. In a small bowl, whisk together the pesto, olive oil, and balsamic vinegar.
2. Season with salt and pepper.

**TO MAKE THE SALAD**
1. In a large bowl, combine the arugula, avocado, and chickpeas.
2. Drizzle the dressing over the salad and gently toss everything together.

**INGREDIENT VARIATION:** To make this salad nut-free, simply omit the walnuts when making the Presto Pesto. Feeling lazy or pressed for time? The refrigerated section of your supermarket has prepared pesto. Use what you need for this recipe, then freeze the rest in ice cube trays to drop into soups and pasta dishes.

PER SERVING: Calories: 390: Total fat: 21g; Protein: 14g; Sodium: 124mg; Fiber: 14g

# ROASTED GARLIC-TOMATO BISQUE

VARIATION ON TOMATO BISQUE

Adding the sweet flavor of roasted garlic to tomato bisque takes it to another level entirely. Top each bowl with a small handful of shredded vegan cheese, and don't skip the basil garnish—the peppery flavor of basil adds a pop of freshness, and it makes this soup pretty enough to serve to company. **SERVINGS: 4**

GLUTEN-FREE
SOY-FREE
BUDGET-FRIENDLY

2 (28-ounce) cans
    crushed tomatoes
1 (28-ounce) can whole peeled
    tomatoes, with juice
1 (15-ounce) can white beans,
    drained and rinsed
½ cup cashew pieces
1 tablespoon dried basil
2 vegetable bouillon cubes
5 Poached Garlic cloves
    (page 20)
3 cups water
Pinch salt
Freshly ground black pepper
2 tablespoons fresh chopped
    basil, for garnish

PREP TIME: 15 MINUTES
COOK TIME: 6 TO 8 HOURS

1. Combine the crushed tomatoes, whole peeled tomatoes, white beans, cashew pieces, dried basil, bouillon cubes, poached garlic, and water in a slow cooker.

2. Cover and cook on low for 6 to 8 hours.

3. Using an immersion blender (or a regular blender, working in batches), blend the soup. Season with salt and pepper.

4. Stir in the fresh basil and serve.

**INGREDIENT TIP:** This bisque pairs perfectly with garlic bread, which is easy to make if you have a batch of Poached Garlic (page 20) in the fridge. Simply spread a few cloves on toasted ciabatta or sourdough bread and sprinkle with salt, pepper, and a drizzle of olive oil. Spice it up with some of the leftover fresh basil.

**PER SERVING:** Calories: 492; Total fat: 9g; Protein: 28g; Sodium: 1,134mg; Fiber: 23g

# CHEESY POTATO-BROCCOLI SOUP

For too long, vegans have watched friends gobble up bowls of cheesy, creamy broccoli soup. Make a batch of this soup when you want to indulge in a big bowl of cheesy comfort. And if you happen to head over to your local bakery and pick up bread bowls to serve this in, even better. **SERVINGS: 4**

GLUTEN-FREE
SOY-FREE
NUT-FREE
BUDGET-FRIENDLY

**2 pounds red or Yukon potatoes, chopped**
**1 (10-ounce) bag frozen broccoli**
**2 cups unsweetened nondairy milk**
**1 small yellow onion, chopped**
**1½ teaspoons minced garlic (3 cloves)**
**3 vegetable bouillon cubes**
**4 cups water**
**1 cup meltable vegan Cheddar-cheese shreds (such as Daiya or Follow Your Heart)**
**Pinch salt**
**Freshly ground black pepper**

PREP TIME: 15 MINUTES
COOK TIME: 5¾ TO 7¾ HOURS

1. Combine the potatoes, broccoli, nondairy milk, onion, garlic, bouillon cubes, and water in a slow cooker; mix well.

2. Cover and cook on low for 5 to 7 hours or on high for 3 to 4 hours.

3. Forty-five minutes before serving, use an immersion blender (or a regular blender, working in batches) to blend the soup until it's nice and creamy.

4. Stir in the vegan cheese, cover, and cook for another 45 minutes.

5. Season with salt and pepper.

**INGREDIENT VARIATION:** I've written the recipes in this chapter with bouillon cubes for convenience, but you can also use Very Easy Vegetable Broth (page 14) or vegetable stock from a can or box. Just eliminate the bouillon cubes and replace the water with the same amount of stock. Be sure to taste and add salt to your liking—you may not need as much when using bouillon cubes or store-bought stock.

**PER SERVING:** Calories: 570; Total fat: 36g; Protein: 11g; Sodium: 831mg; Fiber: 10g

# SPINACH-MUSHROOM SALAD

SERVE WITH CHEESY POTATO-BROCCOLI SOUP

This salad is deceptively easy: it works just as well at a fancier dinner party as it does whipped up quickly and served with soup. The tartness of the lemon juice in the dressing pairs perfectly with the sharp red onion. **SERVINGS: 4**

GLUTEN-FREE
SOY-FREE
NUT-FREE
BUDGET-FRIENDLY

**FOR THE DRESSING**
¼ cup extra-virgin olive oil
¼ cup freshly squeezed
　　lemon juice
1 garlic clove, crushed
Pinch salt
Freshly ground black pepper

**FOR THE SALAD**
1 pound large button
　　mushrooms, thinly sliced
1 (5-ounce) bag baby spinach
⅓ cup chopped fresh flat-leaf
　　parsley
¼ cup thinly sliced red onion

PREP TIME: 10 MINUTES
TOTAL TIME: 15 MINUTES

**TO MAKE THE DRESSING**

1. In a small bowl, whisk together the olive oil, lemon juice, and garlic.

2. Season with salt and pepper.

**TO MAKE THE SALAD**

1. Place the mushrooms in a large salad bowl, and pour the dressing over. Toss to combine and set aside for 5 minutes.

2. Add the spinach, parsley, and red onion to the mushrooms, and toss gently.

**PER SERVING:** Calories: 150; Total fat: 13g; Protein: 5g; Sodium: 79mg; Fiber: 3g

# CREAMY POTATO-VEGETABLE SOUP

VARIATION ON CHEESY POTATO-BROCCOLI SOUP

Your imagination is the limit when you're choosing vegetables to add to this soup. I chose carrots and leeks, but you could also make it with frozen corn or green beans. Try different combinations of vegetables until you find your favorite. If you want to add a little heat to wake up your palate, use vegan pepper Jack cheese. **SERVINGS: 4**

GLUTEN-FREE
SOY-FREE
NUT-FREE
BUDGET-FRIENDLY

2 pounds red or Yukon
    potatoes, chopped
1 (10-ounce) bag
    frozen broccoli
2 cups unsweetened
    nondairy milk
1 leek, washed well, halved
    and sliced
1 small yellow onion, chopped
½ cup fresh or frozen
    diced carrots
2 teaspoons minced garlic
    (4 cloves)
3 vegetable bouillon cubes
4 cups water
1 cup meltable vegan
    Cheddar-cheese shreds
    (such as Daiya or Follow
    Your Heart)
Pinch salt
Freshly ground black pepper

PREP TIME: 15 MINUTES
COOK TIME: 5¾ TO 7¾ HOURS

1.  Combine the potatoes, broccoli, nondairy milk, leek, onion, carrots, garlic, bouillon cubes, and water in a slow cooker; mix well.

2.  Cover and cook on low for 5 to 7 hours or on high for 3 to 4 hours.

3.  Forty-five minutes before serving, use an immersion blender (or a regular blender) to blend half of the soup.

4.  Add the vegan cheese, stir, cover, and cook for 45 minutes.

5.  Season with salt and pepper.

**PER SERVING:** Calories: 635; Total fat: 40g; Protein: 12g; Sodium: 1,722mg; Fiber: 11g

# VEGETABLE STEW

This stew has a little bit of everything—chickpeas, veggies, and spices—for a hearty mix of nutrition and flavor. To power-pack this stew with extra antioxidants, add a generous ¼ teaspoon oregano, thyme, turmeric, or basil. The flavors will blend beautifully, and your body will thank you for providing it with cancer-fighting superpowers. **SERVINGS: 4**

SOY-FREE
NUT-FREE
BUDGET-FRIENDLY

1 (28-ounce) can diced
    tomatoes, with juice
1 (15.5-ounce) can white beans,
    drained and rinsed
1 cup diced green beans
2 medium potatoes, diced
1 cup frozen carrots and
    peas mix
1 small yellow onion, diced
1 (1-inch) piece ginger, peeled
    and minced
1 teaspoon minced garlic
    (2 cloves)
3 cups Very Easy Vegetable
    Broth (page 14) or
    store bought
2 teaspoons ground cumin
½ teaspoon red pepper flakes
Juice of ½ lemon
1 cup dried pasta
Pinch salt
Freshly ground black pepper
Pesto, for serving (Presto
    Pesto, page 132) or
    store bought

PREP TIME: 15 MINUTES
COOK TIME: 6 TO 8 HOURS

1. Combine the diced tomatoes, white beans, green beans, potatoes, carrots and peas mix, onion, ginger, garlic, vegetable broth, cumin, red pepper flakes, and lemon juice in a slow cooker.

2. Cover and cook on low for 6 to 8 hours, or on high for 4 to 5 hours. In the last 20 minutes of cooking, add the pasta and replace the cover.

3. Season with salt and pepper and serve with a dollop of pesto.

**LOVE YOUR LEFTOVERS:** To minimize food waste, cut the entire broccoli stalk into small pieces and throw it into the stew. It will soften, and you won't even notice it's there.

**PER SERVING:** Calories: 386; Total fat: 5g; Protein: 20g; Sodium: 676mg; Fiber: 17g

# BRAISED ENDIVES

Belgian endive is a member of the chicory family. Firm, tightly packed heads of endive stay together when cooked, making them perfect for a warm preparation such as this one. Braising simply means cooking food slowly, covered in a flavored liquid, until it is tender. You can also grill endives, or slice them raw and mix with radicchio and arugula for a classic tricolor salad. **SERVINGS: 4**

GLUTEN-FREE
SOY-FREE
NUT-FREE
BUDGET-FRIENDLY

½ cup water

4 tablespoons unsalted Earth Balance or vegan butter

4 teaspoons brown sugar

3 teaspoons salt

4 medium Belgian endives, stem-end trimmed, quartered lengthwise

PREP TIME: 5 MINUTES
COOK TIME: 6 TO 7 MINUTES

1. In a medium sauté pan with a lid, heat the water, vegan butter, brown sugar, and salt over medium heat, stirring to combine.

2. When the mixture reaches a boil, add the endives to the pan in a single layer. Cover the pan and reduce the heat to medium low. Cook for 6 to 7 minutes, turning once or twice.

**INGREDIENT TIP:** The individual leaves of Belgian endives are shaped like scoops, so they're perfect for serving party foods. You can use them to hold salads or quinoa when you want individual servings that look cute and can be eaten without utensils.

**PER SERVING:** Calories: 132; Total fat: 12g; Protein: 2g; Sodium: 1,904mg; Fiber: 4g

# CURRIED VEGETABLE STEW

VARIATION ON VEGETABLE STEW

Spices and canned coconut milk take a simple vegetable stew to new heights of flavor. Cumin, ginger, and turmeric, found in curry powder, are highly nutritious and full of disease-fighting antioxidants, so don't be afraid to play around and add more if you like your food spicy. **SERVINGS: 4**

GLUTEN-FREE
SOY-FREE
NUT-FREE
BUDGET-FRIENDLY

1 (28-ounce) can diced
    tomatoes, with juice
1 (15-ounce) can chickpeas,
    drained and rinsed
1 (15-ounce) can coconut milk
1 head broccoli, separated
    into florets
2 medium potatoes, diced
1 green bell pepper, diced
1 cup stemmed chopped kale
1 small yellow onion, diced
1 (1-inch) piece ginger, peeled
    and minced
1 teaspoon minced garlic
    (2 cloves)
2 cups Very Easy Vegetable
    Broth (page 14) or
    store bought
2 teaspoons curry powder
2 teaspoons brown sugar
½ teaspoon red pepper flakes
¼ teaspoon ground turmeric
Pinch salt
Cooked brown rice, for serving

PREP TIME: 15 MINUTES
COOK TIME: 6 TO 8 HOURS

1. Combine the diced tomatoes, chickpeas, coconut milk, broccoli, potatoes, bell pepper, kale, onion, ginger, garlic, vegetable broth, curry powder, brown sugar, red pepper flakes, and turmeric in a slow cooker.

2. Cover and cook on low for 6 to 8 hours or on high for 4 to 5 hours.

3. Season with salt, and serve over brown rice.

**INGREDIENT TIP:** Curry powder is a generic term for a variety of spice mixes found in South Asian cuisine. The stuff you find in the spice aisle at your supermarket marked "curry powder" is usually yellow curry powder, which is a great jumping-off point. If you're feeling adventurous, try some others, such as Madras curry, or fiery vindaloo curry for those who like it hot! Shop at an Indian or Asian grocery store, or try making your own.

**PER SERVING:** Calories: 623; Total fat: 30g; Protein: 21g; Sodium: 498mg; Fiber: 20g

# FRIJOLES DE LA OLLA

This brothy Mexican bean stew is incredibly cheap to make, a great source of protein, and totally delicious. You can eat it plain or with a dollop of vegan sour cream and some finely minced white onion and cilantro for garnish. Warmed corn tortillas are nice for soaking up the delicious juices. SERVINGS: 4

GLUTEN-FREE
SOY-FREE
NUT-FREE
BUDGET-FRIENDLY

1 pound dry pinto
    beans, rinsed
1 small yellow onion, diced
1 jalapeño pepper, seeded and
    finely chopped
1½ teaspoons minced garlic
    (3 cloves)
1 tablespoon ground cumin
½ teaspoon Mexican oregano
    (optional)
1 teaspoon red pepper flakes
    (optional)
4 cups water
2 tablespoons salt

PREP TIME: 15 MINUTES
COOK TIME: 6 TO 8 HOURS

1. Place the beans, onion, jalapeño, garlic, cumin, oregano (if using), red pepper flakes (if using), water, and salt in a slow cooker.

2. Cover and cook on low for 6 to 8 hours or on high for 4 to 6 hours.

**LOVE YOUR LEFTOVERS:** If you have leftover stew, you can use the beans as a side dish with tacos, as a burrito filling, or to make a quick dish of rice and beans. If you do this, don't throw out the nutritious bean broth—simply add it to the stock of another soup. If you aren't planning to make soup soon, freeze it until you're ready to use it.

**PER SERVING:** Calories: 417; Total fat: 2g; Protein: 25g; Sodium: 3,513mg; Fiber: 19g

# CORN SALAD WITH CREAMY AVOCADO-LIME DRESSING

SERVE WITH FRIJOLES DE LA OLLA

A little advance planning is required to soak the cashews, but it's worth it for the decadent dressing in this creamy salad inspired by Mexican street corn, or *elote*. Fresh corn is delicious served raw. If you really want to get crazy, grill the corn over a hot grill or grill pan, and add a minced jalapeño for extra heat. **SERVINGS: 4**

GLUTEN-FREE
SOY-FREE
BUDGET-FRIENDLY

**FOR THE DRESSING**
¾ cup raw cashews, soaked for
    at least 7 hours
½ cup fresh cilantro
½ teaspoon minced garlic
    (1 clove)
½ cup water
2½ tablespoons freshly
    squeezed lime juice
½ teaspoon balsamic vinegar
3 tablespoons avocado
Pinch salt

**FOR THE SALAD**
4 ears corn, kernels removed
    from cob
1 small red bell pepper,
    finely diced
1 small green bell pepper,
    finely diced
½ small red onion, finely diced
1 avocado, pitted, peeled,
    and chopped

PREP TIME: 10 MINUTES, PLUS 7 HOURS FOR SOAKING THE CASHEWS

**TO MAKE THE DRESSING**
Place the cashews, cilantro, garlic, water, lime juice, balsamic vinegar, avocado, and salt in a blender, and blend on high until smooth and creamy. Set aside.

**TO MAKE THE SALAD**
In a salad bowl, place the corn, red bell pepper, green bell pepper, onion, and avocado. Drizzle with the dressing and mix thoroughly.

**LOVE YOUR LEFTOVERS:** You'll need about half an avocado to make the dressing. Drizzle the other half with a little lime juice to keep it from browning, then wrap it tightly in plastic wrap and refrigerate.

**INGREDIENT TIP:** When soaking nuts, you'll want to give them a minimum of 7 hours in enough salted water to cover them completely. Soak the cashews overnight, or, if you forgot to do it before bed, just put them in water before you leave for work, and they'll be ready when you get home.

PER SERVING: Calories: 396; Total fat: 28g; Protein: 9g; Sodium: 26mg; Fiber: 9g

# PURÉED BLACK-BEAN SOUP

## VARIATION ON FRIJOLES DE LA OLLA

Black-bean soup is a favorite in so many cultures, and for good reason—it's nutritious, delicious, and inexpensive to make. If you'd like to perk up the flavor, finish it with a squeeze of lemon juice or a spoonful of vinegar. Garnish with a spoonful of Super Simple Salsa (page 128) or, for a classic touch, a thin slice of lemon. **SERVINGS: 4**

GLUTEN-FREE
SOY-FREE
NUT-FREE
BUDGET-FRIENDLY

1 pound dry black
    beans, rinsed
½ yellow onion, diced
½ jalapeño pepper, seeded
    and finely chopped
1 teaspoon minced garlic
    (2 cloves)
1 bay leaf
1 teaspoon dried
    Mexican oregano
1 tablespoon ground cumin
5½ cups water
1½ tablespoons salt

PREP TIME: 15 MINUTES
COOK TIME: 6 TO 8 HOURS

1. Place the black beans, onion, jalapeño, garlic, bay leaf, oregano, cumin, water, and salt in a slow cooker.

2. Cover and cook on low for 6 to 8 hours or on high for 4 to 6 hours.

3. Remove the bay leaf and purée the soup using an immersion blender or a regular blender.

**INGREDIENT VARIATION:** For an American-style black-bean soup, eliminate the jalapeño and cumin, and replace the oregano with an equal amount of dried thyme.

**PER SERVING:** Calories: 401; Total fat: 2g; Protein: 25g; Sodium: 2,635mg; Fiber: 18g

# VEGETABLE HOMINY SOUP

Hominy has a chewy texture that makes this Mexican-inspired vegetable soup a great choice when you want a brothy but hearty soup that's full of bright, fresh flavors. Let everyone garnish their own bowls by passing around a platter of thinly sliced vegetables like scallions, jalapeños, radishes, and red cabbage at the table. **SERVINGS: 4**

GLUTEN-FREE
SOY-FREE
NUT-FREE
BUDGET-FRIENDLY

1 (28-ounce) can
    hominy, drained
1 (28-ounce) can diced
    tomatoes with green chiles
5 medium red or Yukon
    potatoes, diced
1 large yellow onion, diced
2 cups chopped carrots
2 celery stalks, chopped
2 teaspoons minced garlic
    (4 cloves)
2 tablespoons
    chopped cilantro
1½ tablespoons ground cumin
1½ tablespoons seasoned salt
1 tablespoon chili powder
1 bay leaf
4 vegetable bouillon cubes
5 cups water
Pinch salt
Freshly ground black pepper

PREP TIME: 15 MINUTES
COOK TIME: 6 TO 8 HOURS

1. Combine the hominy, diced tomatoes, potatoes, onion, carrots, celery, garlic, cilantro, cumin, seasoned salt, chili powder, bay leaf, vegetable bouillon, and water in a slow cooker; mix well.

2. Cover and cook on low for 6 to 8 hours.

3. Remove the bay leaf. Season with salt and pepper.

**INGREDIENT TIP:** If you've never tried hominy, you're in for a treat! Hominy is corn that has been soaked in an alkali bath, which softens the kernel and causes it to double in size. It's the main ingredient in the Mexican soup pozole. In its dried and ground form, it's used to make tortillas. Buy it canned at your grocery store or specialty market.

PER SERVING: Calories: 427; Total fat: 4g; Protein: 12g; Sodium: 2,881mg; Fiber: 15g

# MEXICAN-INSPIRED SALAD

A spicy avocado dressing is the perfect accent for a protein-packed salad of black beans, quinoa, corn, and fresh veggies. It pairs well with Vegetable Hominy Soup (page 72), but it would be equally good as a side with chili, tacos, or rice and beans. **SERVINGS: 4**

GLUTEN-FREE
SOY-FREE
NUT-FREE
BUDGET-FRIENDLY

**FOR THE DRESSING**
½ avocado, chopped
Juice of 1 large lime
¼ cup olive oil
1 tablespoon finely minced cilantro
1 to 2 teaspoons agave nectar or cane sugar
1 teaspoon hot sauce
½ teaspoon minced garlic (1 clove)
¼ teaspoon ground cumin
Pinch salt
Freshly ground black pepper

**FOR THE SALAD**
1 (5-ounce) bag mixed greens
1 (15-ounce) can black beans, drained and rinsed
1 cup cooked quinoa
1 avocado, pitted, peeled, and chopped
1 medium tomato, diced
½ cup corn kernels
½ red onion, finely diced
½ cup thinly sliced radishes

PREP TIME: 10 MINUTES

**TO MAKE THE DRESSING**
1. In a small bowl, mash the avocado with a fork.
2. Stir in the lime juice, olive oil, cilantro, agave nectar, hot sauce, garlic, and cumin; mix well. Season with salt and pepper.

**TO MAKE THE SALAD**
1. In a large bowl, combine the mixed greens, black beans, quinoa, avocado, tomato, corn kernels, red onion, and radishes.
2. Drizzle the dressing over the salad, and toss one more time to combine.

**INGREDIENT TIP:** To use frozen corn in this salad, place it in a bowl and pour hot water to cover. Let it sit for a minute or so to defrost the corn, then drain and enjoy.

**LOVE YOUR LEFTOVERS:** For a chunky salsa, dice up any remaining avocado, onion, radishes, and tomato, and mix with remaining corn kernels and a sprinkle of salt and pepper. You can store it in the fridge and serve it later with chips.

PER SERVING: Calories: 548; Total fat: 30g; Protein: 17g; Sodium: 94mg; Fiber: 16g

# VEGETABLE BEAN SOUP

VARIATION ON VEGETABLE HOMINY SOUP

Lots of beans make this soup a hearty main dish. To change it up, use sweet potatoes instead of regular potatoes, or add more of your favorite fresh veggies, such as zucchini or bell peppers. For even more fresh flavor, throw in a handful of minced cilantro and a squeeze of fresh lime juice just before serving. SERVINGS: 4

GLUTEN-FREE
SOY-FREE
NUT-FREE
BUDGET-FRIENDLY

1 (28-ounce) can diced
   tomatoes with green chiles
1 (15-ounce) can pinto beans,
   drained and rinsed
1 (15-ounce) can black beans,
   drained and rinsed
1 (15-ounce) can kidney beans,
   drained and rinsed
3 medium red or Yukon
   potatoes, diced
1 large yellow onion, diced
2 cups chopped carrots
2 celery stalks, chopped
2 tablespoons
   chopped cilantro
1½ tablespoons ground cumin
1½ tablespoons seasoned salt
1 tablespoon chili powder
2 teaspoons minced garlic
   (4 cloves)
4 vegetable bouillon cubes
1 cup frozen corn (optional)
5 cups water
Pinch salt
Freshly ground black pepper

PREP TIME: 15 MINUTES
COOK TIME: 6 TO 8 HOURS

1. Combine the diced tomatoes, pinto beans, black beans, kidney beans, potatoes, onion, carrots, celery, cilantro, cumin, seasoned salt, chili powder, garlic, bouillon cubes, corn (if using), and water in a slow cooker; mix well.

2. Cover and cook on low for 6 to 8 hours.

3. Season with salt and pepper.

**TIPS FOR TWO:** This makes a big batch of soup, and you can easily save half to make *fideos*, a Mexican "dry soup" that contains toasted bits of pasta. Reheat your soup over medium-high heat. Toast 1 cup of broken 1-inch pieces of angel hair pasta in a little olive oil until golden, then add the pasta to the boiling soup and simmer until the pasta is tender, about 10 minutes.

**INGREDIENT TIP:** You'll need about 6 medium carrots (the size that generally comes in a bag) to yield 2 cups chopped carrots.

**PER SERVING:** Calories: 775; Total fat: 4g; Protein: 42g; Sodium: 2,479mg; Fiber: 33g

# LENTIL-QUINOA CHILI

This chili is a super satisfying cold-weather meal. Protein from the lentils, black beans, and quinoa will leave you feeling full and satisfied. If you want to vary this recipe, try adding additional spices, such as ground coriander or cayenne pepper. Feeling adventurous? Stir in a little grated unsweetened chocolate, too. **SERVINGS: 4**

GLUTEN-FREE
SOY-FREE
NUT-FREE
BUDGET-FRIENDLY

½ cup dry green or brown
   lentils, rinsed
1 (15-ounce) can black beans,
   drained and rinsed
⅓ cup uncooked
   quinoa, rinsed
1 small yellow onion, diced
2 medium carrots, diced
2 teaspoons ground cumin
2 teaspoons chili powder
1½ teaspoons minced garlic
   (3 cloves)
1 teaspoon dried oregano
3 vegetable bouillon cubes
1 bay leaf
4 cups water
Pinch salt

PREP TIME: 15 MINUTES
COOK TIME: 7 TO 9 HOURS

1.  Place the lentils, black beans, quinoa, onion, carrots, cumin, chili powder, garlic, oregano, bouillon cubes, bay leaf, and water in a slow cooker; mix well.

2.  Cover and cook on low for 7 to 9 hours or on high for 4 to 5 hours.

3.  Remove the bay leaf, season with salt, and serve.

**TIPS FOR TWO:** To enjoy this twice, serve smaller portions over baked sweet potatoes. Garnish with a dollop of vegan sour cream and some sliced scallions for an amazing stuffed baked potato entrée.

PER SERVING: Calories: 372; Total fat: 3g; Protein: 22g; Sodium: 547mg; Fiber: 19g

# CUCUMBER-DILL SALAD WITH LEMON DRESSING

SERVE WITH LENTIL-QUINOA CHILI

The fresh flavors of cucumber and dill combine with a traditional French-style vinaigrette for a versatile salad that you can enjoy with just about any recipe in this book. If you don't like dill, or to vary your salad repertoire, try using fresh parsley instead. **SERVINGS: 4**

GLUTEN-FREE
SOY-FREE
NUT-FREE
BUDGET-FRIENDLY

**FOR THE DRESSING**
¼ cup red wine vinegar
2 tablespoons freshly
    squeezed lemon juice
1 tablespoon Dijon mustard
1 teaspoon fresh or
    dried thyme
½ teaspoon minced garlic
    (1 clove)
½ teaspoon agave nectar or
    cane sugar (optional)
½ cup olive oil
Pinch salt
Freshly ground black pepper

**FOR THE SALAD**
3 cucumbers, chopped
½ cup minced fresh dill
3 scallions, thinly sliced
Pinch salt

**PREP TIME: 10 MINUTES**

**TO MAKE THE DRESSING**

1. In a small bowl, whisk together the vinegar, lemon juice, Dijon mustard, thyme, garlic, and agave nectar (if using).

2. Slowly drizzle in the olive oil, whisking constantly to combine. Season with salt and pepper.

**TO MAKE THE SALAD**

1. Combine the cucumbers, dill, and scallions in a large bowl.

2. Drizzle the dressing over the cucumbers and toss to combine. Season with salt.

**INGREDIENT TIP:** If you're planning to make this salad ahead of time, drain the cucumbers so the salad doesn't become watery. Place the cucumbers in a strainer, sprinkle with a little salt, and let stand for 10 minutes. Rinse with cold water, pat dry, and proceed with the recipe. Your cucumbers will stay fresh and crunchy.

**PER SERVING:** Calories: 280; Total fat: 26g; Protein: 3g; Sodium: 143mg; Fiber: 3g

# LENTIL-SWEET POTATO CHILI

VARIATION ON LENTIL-QUINOA CHILI

Cinnamon is the perfect companion to sweet potato, and that flavor combination is what makes this chili special. Serve hot bowls of this chili garnished with toasted pumpkin seeds and a spoonful of vegan sour cream. If you like a little extra heat, try adding a diced poblano chile to this recipe.  SERVINGS: 4

GLUTEN-FREE
SOY-FREE
NUT-FREE
BUDGET-FRIENDLY

½ cup dry brown or green
    lentils, rinsed
1 (15-ounce) can black beans,
    drained and rinsed
1 (15-ounce) can pinto beans,
    drained and rinsed
1 cup frozen sweet potato
1 small yellow onion, diced
2 medium carrots, diced
1½ teaspoons minced garlic
    (3 cloves)
2 teaspoons ground cumin
2 teaspoons chili powder
½ teaspoon ground cinnamon
1 teaspoon dried oregano
3 vegetable bouillon cubes
1 bay leaf
4 cups water
Pinch salt

PREP TIME: 15 MINUTES
COOK TIME: 7 TO 9 HOURS

1. Place the lentils, black beans, pinto beans, sweet potato, onion, carrots, garlic, cumin, chili powder, cinnamon, oregano, bouillon cubes, bay leaf, and water in a slow cooker; mix well.

2. Cover and cook on low for 7 to 9 hours or on high for 4 to 5 hours.

3. Remove the bay leaf, and season with the salt.

PER SERVING: Calories: 539; Total fat: 3g; Protein: 32g; Sodium: 570mg; Fiber: 28g

# EGGPLANT CURRY

This is a great recipe to make in the summer, when eggplant and zucchini are in season and available at your local farmers' market for very little money. Serve it with basmati rice and some heated naan bread. If you're feeling ambitious, stir in some finely chopped mango and cilantro into plain vegan yogurt for a cooling garnish called *raita* that is absolutely fabulous with curried vegetables.  **SERVINGS: 4**

GLUTEN-FREE
SOY-FREE
NUT-FREE
BUDGET-FRIENDLY

5 cups chopped eggplant

4 cups chopped zucchini

2 cups stemmed and chopped kale

1 (15-ounce) can full-fat coconut milk

1 (14.5-ounce) can diced tomatoes, drained

1 (6-ounce) can tomato paste

1 medium yellow onion, chopped

2 teaspoons minced garlic (4 cloves)

1 tablespoon curry powder

1 tablespoon garam masala

¼ teaspoon cayenne pepper

¼ teaspoon ground cumin

1 teaspoon salt

Cooked rice, for serving

**PREP TIME: 15 MINUTES**
**COOK TIME: 6 TO 8 HOURS**

1. Combine the eggplant, zucchini, kale, coconut milk, diced tomatoes, tomato paste, onion, garlic, curry powder, garam masala, cayenne pepper, cumin, and salt in a slow cooker; mix well.

2. Cover and cook on low for 6 to 8 hours or on high for 4 to 5 hours.

3. Serve over rice.

**INGREDIENT TIP:** You'll need an eggplant that weighs about 1¼ pounds to yield 5 cups chopped eggplant, and about 5 medium zucchini for 4 cups chopped zucchini.

........................................................

**PER SERVING:** Calories: 417; Total fat: 27g; Protein: 11g; Sodium: 683mg; Fiber: 17g

# INDIAN-INSPIRED SALAD

SERVE WITH EGGPLANT CURRY

Peanuts add crunch and flavor to this fun salad. The lime juice in the dressing provides a zesty counterpoint to the richness of curry dishes made with coconut milk. For best results, toss this fast salad together just before you serve it. **SERVINGS: 4**

GLUTEN-FREE
SOY-FREE
BUDGET-FRIENDLY

2 cucumbers, peeled, seeded, and cut into 1-inch sticks
1 small red onion, diced
2 medium tomatoes, diced
2 jalapeño peppers, seeded and diced
Juice of 2 limes
1½ tablespoons canola or other neutral-flavored oil
3½ tablespoons chopped roasted peanuts
½ teaspoon ground coriander
¼ teaspoon chili powder
¼ teaspoon ground cumin
Pinch salt
Freshly ground black pepper

PREP TIME: 10 MINUTES

1. Place the cucumbers, red onion, tomatoes, jalapeños, lime juice, oil, peanuts, coriander, chili powder, and cumin in a salad bowl; mix thoroughly.

2. Season with salt and pepper.

**PER SERVING:** Calories: 143; Total fat: 10g; Protein: 4g; Sodium: 44mg; Fiber: 3g

# BUTTERNUT SQUASH CURRY

VARIATION ON EGGPLANT CURRY

Butternut squash and sweet potato add a sweetness to this curry that offsets the heat of the cayenne pepper. If you don't feel like peeling squash, use 4 cups pre-prepped or frozen butternut squash instead. **SERVINGS: 4**

GLUTEN-FREE
SOY-FREE
NUT-FREE
BUDGET-FRIENDLY

1 large butternut squash, peeled and chopped into cubes

1 small sweet potato, peeled and chopped

2 cups stemmed and chopped kale

1 (15-ounce) can diced tomatoes, drained

1 (15-ounce) can full-fat coconut milk

1 (6-ounce) can tomato paste

1 medium yellow onion

2 teaspoons minced garlic (4 cloves)

1 tablespoon curry powder

1 tablespoon garam masala

¼ teaspoon cayenne pepper

¼ teaspoon ground cumin

1 teaspoon salt

Cooked rice, for serving

PREP TIME: 15 MINUTES
COOK TIME: 6 TO 8 HOURS

1. Combine the butternut squash, sweet potato, kale, diced tomatoes, coconut milk, tomato paste, onion, garlic, curry powder, garam masala, cayenne pepper, cumin, and salt in a slow cooker; mix well.

2. Cover and cook on low for 6 to 8 hours or on high for 4 to 5 hours.

3. Serve over rice.

**PER SERVING:** Calories: 394; Total fat: 26g; Protein: 8g; Sodium: 677mg; Fiber: 9g

# MEATY CHILI

Vegetables are great, and we all love them, but sometimes you want a chili that tastes like its meaty, not-at-all-vegan cousin. Veggie crumbles are the answer, and they can be found in the frozen-foods aisle of any grocery store. Make this one when you're feeling nostalgic. SERVINGS: 4

NUT-FREE
BUDGET-FRIENDLY

PREP TIME: 15 MINUTES
COOK TIME: 6 TO 8 HOURS

1 tablespoon olive oil

2 (11-ounce) packages of faux-ground-beef veggie crumbles (such as Beyond Meat)

1 large red onion, chopped

1 large jalapeño pepper, seeded and chopped

2½ teaspoons minced garlic (5 cloves)

1 (28-ounce) can diced tomatoes, with juice

1 (15-ounce) can kidney beans, drained and rinsed

1 (15-ounce) can black beans, drained and rinsed

½ cup frozen corn

¼ cup chili powder

2 tablespoons ground cumin

1 teaspoon smoked paprika

1 vegetable bouillon cube

1½ cups water

1. Heat the olive oil in a sauté pan over medium-high heat. Add the veggie crumbles, onion, jalapeño, and garlic, and cook for 3 to 4 minutes, stirring occasionally.

2. Combine the veggie-crumble mixture, diced tomatoes, kidney beans, black beans, frozen corn, chili powder, cumin, smoked paprika, bouillon cube, and water in a slow cooker; mix well.

3. Cover and cook on low for 6 to 8 hours.

**INGREDIENT TIP:** To save time, sauté the veggie crumbles and vegetables the night before and store them in a plastic container in the refrigerator to use in the morning.

**PER SERVING:** Calories: 608; Total fat: 14g; Protein: 41g; Sodium: 282mg; Fiber: 24g

# ROMAINE SALAD WITH RASPBERRY VINAIGRETTE

SERVE WITH MEATY CHILI

Dress up your salad with this sweet raspberry vinaigrette. Change it up by using baby greens instead of romaine, or some toasted slivered almonds instead of sunflower seeds. **SERVINGS: 4**

GLUTEN-FREE
SOY-FREE
NUT-FREE
BUDGET-FRIENDLY

**FOR THE DRESSING**
1½ cups raspberries
⅓ cup red wine vinegar
¼ cup olive oil
1½ tablespoons sugar
1½ teaspoons grated
    lemon zest
Pinch salt
Freshly ground black pepper

**FOR THE SALAD**
1 package romaine
    hearts, chopped
10 to 15 cherry
    tomatoes, halved
1 small cucumber, diced
½ cup dried cranberries
½ cup unsalted
    sunflower seeds

**PREP TIME: 10 MINUTES**

**TO MAKE THE DRESSING**
1. Purée the raspberries in a blender or food processor.
2. Combine the raspberry purée with the red wine vinegar, olive oil, sugar, and lemon zest. Season with salt and pepper.

**TO MAKE THE SALAD**
In a large bowl, gently combine the romaine hearts, cherry tomatoes, cucumber, dried cranberries, sunflower seeds, and raspberry vinaigrette. Serve immediately.

**COOKING TIP:** If you have a microplane grater, it's easy to rub the zest (yellow part) of the lemon peel from the lemon. If you don't have one, use a sharp paring knife to carefully peel away just the yellow part of the lemon peel. Use the knife to scrape the bitter white pith from the peel, then mince it finely.

**PER SERVING:** Calories: 296; Total fat: 17g; Protein: 7g; Sodium: 68mg; Fiber: 10g

# SKYLINE CHILI

VARIATION ON MEATY CHILI

Skyline Chili is also known as Cincinnati Chili, and anyone from Ohio knows that it's not your average chili dish. This unique chili is usually served over spaghetti or sometimes even hot dogs! Serve it on its own or over cooked pasta, or spoon it onto veggie dogs with some finely chopped onion if you want to serve something fun at your next cookout. **SERVINGS: 4**

NUT-FREE
BUDGET-FRIENDLY

PREP TIME: 15 MINUTES
COOK TIME: 6 TO 8 HOURS

1 tablespoon olive oil

3 (11-ounce) packages faux-ground-beef veggie crumbles (such as Beyond Meat)

1 (14.5-ounce) can tomato sauce

1⅓ (6-ounce) cans tomato paste

¼ cup chili powder

1¼ teaspoons salt

1 tablespoon distilled white vinegar

2 teaspoons A1 sauce

2 teaspoons ground cinnamon

1 teaspoon ground allspice

1 teaspoon onion salt

1 teaspoon freshly ground black pepper

¼ teaspoon garlic powder

1 vegetable bouillon cube

1 cup water

1. Heat the olive oil in a sauté pan over medium-high heat. Sauté the veggie crumbles for 3 to 4 minutes.

2. Combine the veggie crumbles, tomato sauce, tomato paste, chili powder, salt, white vinegar, A1 sauce, cinnamon, allspice, onion salt, black pepper, garlic powder, bouillon cube, and water in a slow cooker; mix mix well.

3. Cover and cook on low for 6 to 8 hours.

**PER SERVING:** Calories: 297; Total fat: 15g; Protein: 24g; Sodium: 1,928mg; Fiber: 9g

# SWEET POTATO BISQUE

This recipe is sweet, spiced, and so easy to throw together. If you're really in a rush, use frozen diced sweet potatoes instead of fresh. Try garnishing this creamy bisque with a swirl of vegan sour cream. A spoonful of Presto Pesto (page 132) would make it even more special. SERVINGS: 4

GLUTEN-FREE
SOY-FREE
NUT-FREE
BUDGET-FRIENDLY

2 sweet potatoes, peeled
    and sliced
2 cups frozen
    butternut squash
2 (14.5-ounce) cans full-fat
    coconut milk
1 medium yellow onion, sliced
1 teaspoon minced garlic
    (2 cloves)
1 tablespoon dried basil
1 tablespoon chili powder
1 tablespoon ground cumin
½ cup water
Pinch salt
Freshly ground black pepper

PREP TIME: 15 MINUTES
COOK TIME: 8 HOURS

1. Combine the sweet potatoes, butternut squash, coconut milk, onion, garlic, dried basil, chili powder, cumin, and water in a slow cooker; mix well.

2. Cover and cook on low for 8 hours or on high for 4 to 6 hours.

3. Using an immersion blender (or a regular blender, working in batches), blend the soup until it's nice and creamy.

4. Season with salt and pepper.

**LOVE YOUR LEFTOVERS:** If you have extra sweet potatoes, slice them into thin rounds (¼ inch thick) and bake them in the oven at 400 degrees for 25 to 30 minutes, until they're soft and chewy. Keep these on hand for the next time you're hungry for a healthy snack. (Did you know that sweet potatoes are one of the healthiest foods on the planet?)

PER SERVING: Calories: 662; Total fat: 50g; Protein: 8g; Sodium: 106mg; Fiber: 12g

# MIXED GREENS WITH TARRAGON DRESSING

SERVE WITH SWEET POTATO BISQUE

Don't be fooled by this salad's simple name: it's much more than greens and dressing. A perfect balance of tangy, crunchy, sweet, and spicy, the salad balances the peppery Dijon dressing with crisp croutons, chopped dates, and smooth avocado. **SERVINGS: 4**

SOY-FREE
NUT-FREE
BUDGET-FRIENDLY

**FOR THE DRESSING**

2 tablespoons olive oil

Zest and juice of 1 lemon

1 tablespoon agave nectar

1 teaspoon Dijon mustard

¼ teaspoon salt

¼ teaspoon freshly ground
    black pepper

Leaves from 4 fresh tarragon
    sprigs, chopped

**FOR THE SALAD**

1 (5-ounce) bag mixed
    spring greens

½ cup chopped dates

½ cup dry-roasted salted
    pumpkin seeds

1 avocado, cut into
    bite-size pieces

Croutons (see tip)
    or store bought

PREP TIME: 10 MINUTES

**TO MAKE THE DRESSING**

In a small bowl, whisk together the olive oil, lemon zest and juice, agave nectar, Dijon mustard, salt, pepper, and tarragon until well combined.

**TO MAKE THE SALAD**

1. Place the greens, dates, pumpkin seeds, and avocado in a large bowl.

2. Drizzle the dressing over the salad, toss to combine, and garnish with croutons.

**INGREDIENT TIP:** If you want to make your own croutons, cut a day-old French baguette into bite-size squares, and toss on a rimmed baking sheet with 2 tablespoons olive oil, a dash of garlic salt, and coarsely ground black pepper. Spread in an even layer and bake at 400 degrees for 10 minutes, or until golden brown.

PER SERVING: Calories: 341; Total fat: 25g; Protein: 6g; Sodium: 171mg; Fiber: 7g

# PROTEIN-PACKED SWEET POTATO BISQUE

VARIATION ON SWEET POTATO BISQUE

Add extra protein and creaminess to your bisque recipe by using white beans and cashews. Once it's puréed, you'll swear it contains real cream. **SERVINGS: 4**

GLUTEN-FREE
SOY-FREE
BUDGET-FRIENDLY

2 sweet potatoes, peeled
    and sliced
2 cups frozen
    butternut squash
2 (15-ounce) cans full-fat
    coconut milk
½ cup cashews
1 (15-ounce) can white beans,
    drained and rinsed
1 medium yellow onion, sliced
1 teaspoon minced garlic
    (2 cloves)
1 tablespoon dried basil
1 tablespoon chili powder
1 tablespoon ground cumin
1 vegetable bouillon cube
1 cup water

PREP TIME: 15 MINUTES
COOK TIME: 8 HOURS

1. Combine the sweet potatoes, butternut squash, coconut milk, cashews, white beans, onion, garlic, dried basil, chili powder, cumin, bouillon cube, and water in a slow cooker; mix well.

2. Cover and cook on low for 8 hours or on high for 4 to 6 hours.

3. Use an immersion blender (or a regular blender, working in batches) to blend the soup until it's nice and creamy.

**PER SERVING:** Calories: 967; Total fat: 60g; Protein: 24g; Sodium: 234mg; Fiber: 21g

# CARROT-GINGER SOUP

With this recipe, you'll never have to pay outrageous prices for fancy carrot-ginger soup from an expensive grocery store ever again! Make a batch of this delicious vegan staple, and freeze it in small portions so you can have it whenever you're in the mood. It's great on its own, sipped hot from a cup, or as a meal with a Fall Apple-Spinach Salad (page 88). **SERVINGS: 4**

GLUTEN-FREE
SOY-FREE
NUT-FREE
BUDGET-FRIENDLY

**2 (10-ounce) packages frozen carrots**
**2 (14.5-ounce) cans diced tomatoes, with juice**
**1 medium yellow onion, diced**
**1 (1-inch) piece fresh ginger, peeled and minced**
**1½ teaspoons minced garlic (3 cloves)**
**Zest and juice of 1 lemon**
**2 vegetable bouillon cubes**
**3½ cups water**
**2 tablespoons vegan sour cream**
**Pinch salt**
**Freshly ground black pepper**

PREP TIME: 15 MINUTES
COOK TIME: 5 TO 6 HOURS

1. Combine the carrots, diced tomatoes, onion, ginger, garlic, lemon zest and juice, bouillon cubes, and water in a slow cooker; mix well.

2. Cover and cook on low for 5 to 6 hours.

3. Purée using an immersion blender (or with a regular blender, working in batches).

4. Stir in the vegan sour cream and season with salt and pepper.

**PER SERVING:** Calories: 138; Total fat: 2g; Protein: 4g; Sodium: 468mg; Fiber: 7g

# FALL APPLE-SPINACH SALAD

SERVE WITH CARROT-GINGER SOUP

This is a classic fall salad, with cranberries, apples, and walnuts. The sweetness of the fruit in this dish complements the spiciness of the ginger in the Carrot-Ginger Soup really nicely. With a side of crusty French bread, you have a full fall menu. **SERVINGS: 4**

GLUTEN-FREE
SOY-FREE
BUDGET-FRIENDLY

**FOR THE DRESSING**
4 tablespoons olive oil
¼ cup apple cider vinegar
1 tablespoon maple syrup
1 teaspoon Dijon mustard
Pinch salt
Freshly ground black pepper

**FOR THE SALAD**
1 (5-ounce) package
   baby spinach
1 red apple, cored and sliced
1 green apple, cored and sliced
¾ cup chopped walnuts
½ cup dried cranberries

PREP TIME: 10 MINUTES

**TO MAKE THE DRESSING**
In a small bowl, whisk together the olive oil, vinegar, maple syrup, and Dijon mustard until combined. Season with salt and pepper.

**TO MAKE THE SALAD**
1. Place the baby spinach, apples, walnuts, and dried cranberries in a large bowl.
2. Drizzle the dressing over the salad, toss, and serve.

**LOVE YOUR LEFTOVERS:** Spinach is one of those greens you can eat even when it's wilted, so feel free to double this salad and enjoy it for lunch the next day.

**PER SERVING:** Calories: 356; Total fat: 28g; Protein: 7g; Sodium: 84mg; Fiber: 6g

# CARROT-LEMONGRASS SOUP

VARIATION ON CARROT-GINGER SOUP

Lemongrass gives this soup a delicious Southeast Asian flavor. If you have some chili garlic sauce in the refrigerator, a swirl in each bowl is a delicious topping. A little minced fresh cilantro would be nice, too. **SERVINGS: 4**

GLUTEN-FREE
SOY-FREE
NUT-FREE
BUDGET-FRIENDLY

2 (10-ounce) packages
    frozen carrots
2 (14.5-ounce) cans diced
    tomatoes, with juice
1 medium yellow onion, diced
1 (2-inch) piece fresh
    lemongrass, pounded
    and minced
1½ teaspoons minced garlic
    (3 cloves)
Zest and juice of 1 lemon
2 vegetable bouillon cubes
3½ cups water
2 tablespoons vegan
    sour cream
Pinch salt
Freshly ground black pepper

PREP TIME: 15 MINUTES
COOK TIME: 5 TO 6 HOURS

1. Combine the carrots, diced tomatoes, onion, lemongrass, garlic, lemon zest and juice, bouillon cubes, and water in a slow cooker; mix well.

2. Cover and cook on low for 5 to 6 hours.

3. Purée using an immersion blender (or a regular blender, working in batches).

4. Stir in the vegan sour cream, and season with salt and pepper.

**PER SERVING:** Calories: 134; Total fat: 2g; Protein: 4g; Sodium: 470mg; Fiber: 7g

African Sweet Potato Stew (page 100)

# CHAPTER FOUR
# STAND-ALONE SUPPERS

# ALOO GOBI

Aloo gobi is a traditional vegetarian dish that you can often find at Nepalese, Pakistani, or Indian restaurants. It's also known as "cauliflower and potatoes." If you don't like your food too spicy, turn down the heat in this dish by removing the seeds from the jalapeño before cooking. SERVINGS: 4

GLUTEN-FREE
SOY-FREE
NUT-FREE
BUDGET-FRIENDLY

1 large cauliflower, cut into 1-inch pieces
1 large russet potato, peeled and diced
1 medium yellow onion, peeled and diced
1 cup canned diced tomatoes, with juice
1 cup frozen peas
¼ cup water
1 (2-inch) piece fresh ginger, peeled and finely chopped
1½ teaspoons minced garlic (3 cloves)
1 jalapeño pepper, stemmed and sliced
1 tablespoon cumin seeds
1 tablespoon garam masala
1 teaspoon ground turmeric
1 heaping tablespoon fresh cilantro
Cooked rice, for serving (optional)

PREP TIME: 15 MINUTES
COOK TIME: 4 TO 5 HOURS

1. Combine the cauliflower, potato, onion, diced tomatoes, peas, water, ginger, garlic, jalapeño, cumin seeds, garam masala, and turmeric in a slow cooker; mix until well combined.

2. Cover and cook on low for 4 to 5 hours.

3. Garnish with the cilantro, and serve over cooked rice (if using).

**INGREDIENT VARIATION:** You can swap the fresh ginger and garlic for dried varieties. I love to keep a full range of spices on hand so I'm less reliant on fresh ingredients. And don't worry—most of the nutritional benefits stay intact when spices are dried!

PER SERVING: Calories: 115; Total fat: <1g; Protein: 6g; Sodium: 62mg; Fiber: 6g

# JACKFRUIT CARNITAS

Jackfruit is a giant, weird-looking fruit that grows in the southern parts of Asia. Because of its texture, it has recently become a popular alternative to meat, and works great in recipes that typically call for shredded pork or chicken. Jackfruit can be found online, but is also available canned in grocery stores. Do be sure that you're buying jackfruit packed in water, as it's sometimes also packed in syrup for sweet applications. SERVINGS: 4

GLUTEN-FREE
SOY-FREE
NUT-FREE
BUDGET-FRIENDLY

2 (20-ounce) cans
    jackfruit, drained, hard
    pieces discarded
¾ cup Very Easy Vegetable
    Broth (page 14) or
    store bought
1 tablespoon ground cumin
1 tablespoon dried oregano
1½ teaspoons
    ground coriander
1 teaspoon minced garlic
    (2 cloves)
½ teaspoon ground cinnamon
2 bay leaves
Tortillas, for serving
Optional toppings: diced
    onions, sliced radishes,
    fresh cilantro, lime wedges,
    Nacho Cheese (page 125)

PREP TIME: 15 MINUTES
COOK TIME: 8 HOURS

1. Combine the jackfruit, vegetable broth, cumin, oregano, coriander, garlic, cinnamon, and bay leaves in a slow cooker. Stir to combine.

2. Cover and cook on low for 8 hours or on high for 4 hours.

3. Use two forks to pull the jackfruit apart into shreds.

4. Remove the bay leaves. Serve in warmed tortillas with your favorite taco fixings.

**INGREDIENT TIP:** If you have some extra time, the jackfruit carnitas are even more flavorful when sautéed with a little bit of oil prior to putting them in the slow cooker.

**LOVE YOUR LEFTOVERS:** Got leftovers? Jackfruit carnitas are delicious in burritos, atop a bed of rice and beans, in sandwiches, on pizza, and more. Have fun getting creative—the sky's the limit!

PER SERVING: Calories: 286; Total fat: 2g; Protein: 6g; Sodium: 155mg; Fiber: 5g

# BAKED BEANS

Despite its name, this dish is usually stewed rather than baked. You can eat these beans on their own, garnished with some chopped scallions and a dollop of vegan sour cream. Alternatively, put them in your breakfast burrito, or mash them as a sandwich filling and serve with your favorite fixings. SERVINGS: 4

GLUTEN-FREE
NUT-FREE
BUDGET-FRIENDLY

2 (15-ounce) cans white beans, drained and rinsed
1 (15-ounce) can tomato sauce
1 medium yellow onion, finely diced
1½ teaspoons minced garlic (3 cloves)
3 tablespoons brown sugar
2 tablespoons molasses
1 tablespoon prepared yellow mustard
1 tablespoon chili powder
1 teaspoon soy sauce
Pinch salt
Freshly ground black pepper

PREP TIME: 15 MINUTES
COOK TIME: 6 HOURS

1. Place the beans, tomato sauce, onion, garlic, brown sugar, molasses, mustard, chili powder, and soy sauce into a slow cooker; mix well.

2. Cover and cook on low for 6 hours. Season with salt and pepper before serving.

**INGREDIENT VARIATION:** One of my recipe testers suggested this would be good cooked with ½ tablespoon imitation bacon bits for an extra smoky flavor. For a healthier option, try adding 1 teaspoon smoked paprika.

**PER SERVING:** Calories: 468; Total fat: 2g; Protein: 28g; Sodium: 714mg; Fiber: 20g

# BRUSSELS SPROUTS CURRY

This recipe is adapted from one that my friend Renee posted on the blog *Plant Based on a Budget*. It's great to make in winter when Brussels sprouts are in season here in California. At the farmers' market, I can buy all the produce I need to make this recipe for $5 or less.  SERVINGS: 4

BUDGET-FRIENDLY

¾ pound Brussels sprouts, bottoms cut off and sliced in half
1 can full-fat coconut milk
1 cup Very Easy Vegetable Broth (page 14) or store bought
1 medium onion, diced
1 medium carrot, thinly sliced
1 medium red or Yukon potato, diced
1½ teaspoons minced garlic (3 cloves)
1 (1-inch) piece fresh ginger, peeled and minced
1 small serrano chile, seeded and finely chopped
2 tablespoons peanut butter
1 tablespoon rice vinegar or other vinegar
1 tablespoon cane sugar or agave nectar
1 tablespoon soy sauce
1 teaspoon curry powder
1 teaspoon ground turmeric
Pinch salt
Freshly ground black pepper
Cooked rice, for serving (optional)

PREP TIME: 15 MINUTES
COOK TIME: 7 TO 8 HOURS

1. Place the Brussels sprouts, coconut milk, vegetable broth, onion, carrot, potato, garlic, ginger, serrano chile, peanut butter, vinegar, cane sugar, soy sauce, curry powder, and turmeric in a slow cooker. Mix well.

2. Cover and cook on low for 7 to 8 hours or on high for 4 to 5 hours.

3. Season with salt and pepper. Serve over rice (if using).

**INGREDIENT VARIATION:** As written, this is a soupy curry that's best when served over rice. It's also good served over quinoa, or as a soup with some naan bread. If you'd like a heartier stew, add some peas, more potato, or more Brussels sprouts.

**PER SERVING:** Calories: 404; Total fat: 29g; Protein: 10g; Sodium: 544mg; Fiber: 8g

# JAMBALAYA

While writing this book, I discovered how much I love food from the South. This is another dish from Louisiana, with influences from Spanish and French cuisine. It's traditionally made with sausage, and if you can, I recommend following my tip below for some additional texture. SERVINGS: 4

GLUTEN-FREE
SOY-FREE
NUT-FREE
BUDGET-FRIENDLY

2 cups Very Easy Vegetable
    Broth (page 14) or
    store bought
1 large yellow onion, diced
1 green bell pepper, seeded
    and chopped
2 celery stalks, chopped
1½ teaspoons minced garlic
    (3 cloves)
1 (15-ounce) can dark red
    kidney beans, drained
    and rinsed
1 (15-ounce) can black-eyed
    peas, drained and rinsed
1 (15-ounce) can diced
    tomatoes, drained
2 tablespoons Cajun seasoning
2 teaspoons dried oregano
2 teaspoons dried parsley
1 teaspoon cayenne pepper
1 teaspoon smoked paprika
½ teaspoon dried thyme
Cooked rice, for serving
    (optional)

PREP TIME: 15 MINUTES
COOK TIME: 6 TO 8 HOURS

1. Combine the vegetable broth, onion, bell pepper, celery, garlic, kidney beans, black-eyed peas, diced tomatoes, Cajun seasoning, oregano, parsley, cayenne pepper, smoked paprika, and dried thyme in a slow cooker; mix well.

2. Cover and cook on low for 6 to 8 hours.

3. Serve over rice (if using).

**INGREDIENT VARIATION:** Jambalaya is traditionally made with meat. For extra flavor and protein, try adding some sautéed vegan sausage slices to the cooked jambalaya.

**LOVE YOUR LEFTOVERS:** When you drain the liquid from the diced tomatoes, you can save it in the freezer or refrigerator to add to soups or use to flavor rice.

PER SERVING: Calories: 428; Total fat: 2g; Protein: 28g; Sodium: 484mg; Fiber: 19g

# MUSHROOM-KALE STROGANOFF

Stroganoff is a Russian dish that is traditionally made with beef. In this healthier version, you can use your favorite mushrooms, such as button, cremini, or more exotic types if you're feeling adventurous. It's most commonly served over noodles, but you can also serve it over brown rice or quinoa. SERVINGS: 4

SOY-FREE
NUT-FREE
BUDGET-FRIENDLY

1 pound mushrooms, sliced
1½ cups Very Easy Vegetable
    Broth (page 14) or
    store bought
1 cup stemmed and
    chopped kale
1 small yellow onion, diced
2 garlic cloves, minced
2 tablespoons
    all-purpose flour
2 tablespoons ketchup or
    tomato paste
2 teaspoons paprika
½ cup vegan sour cream
¼ cup chopped fresh parsley
Cooked rice, pasta, or quinoa,
    for serving

PREP TIME: 15 MINUTES
COOK TIME: 6 TO 8 HOURS

1. Combine the mushrooms, vegetable broth, kale, onion, garlic, flour, ketchup or tomato paste, and paprika in a slow cooker. Mix thoroughly.

2. Cover and cook on low for 6 to 8 hours.

3. Stir in the sour cream and parsley just before serving.

4. Serve over rice, pasta, or quinoa.

**INGREDIENT VARIATION:** Instead of kale, use any type of greens you have on hand, such as spinach or Swiss chard.

**PER SERVING:** Calories: 146; Total fat: 7g; Protein: 8g; Sodium: 417mg; Fiber: 3g

# SLOPPY JOE FILLING

Textured vegetable protein, also known as TVP, is an alternative to meat that became popular in the 1970s. It's got a higher protein content than meat without all the bad stuff that comes with eating meat, like hormones, carcinogens, and cholesterol. Plus it really brings this Sloppy Joe filling together! SERVINGS: 4

NUT-FREE
BUDGET-FRIENDLY

PREP TIME: 15 MINUTES
COOK TIME: 6 TO 8 HOURS

3 cups textured
   vegetable protein
3 cups water
2 (6-ounce) cans tomato paste,
   or 1 cup ketchup
1 medium yellow onion, diced
½ medium green bell pepper,
   finely diced
2 teaspoons minced garlic
   (4 cloves)
4 tablespoons vegan
   Worcestershire sauce
3 tablespoons brown sugar
3 tablespoons apple
   cider vinegar
3 tablespoons prepared
   yellow mustard
2 tablespoons hot sauce
   (optional)
1 tablespoon salt
1 teaspoon chili powder
Sliced, toasted buns or cooked
   rice, for serving

1. Combine the textured vegetable protein, water, tomato paste, onion, bell pepper, garlic, Worcestershire sauce, brown sugar, vinegar, mustard, hot sauce (if using), salt, and chili powder in a slow cooker. Mix well.

2. Cover and cook on low for 6 to 8 hours or on high for 4 to 5 hours.

3. Serve on sliced, toasted buns or over rice.

**INGREDIENT TIP:** If it's not sloppy enough for you, add more ketchup when serving. While ketchup gives Sloppy Joes their traditional flavor, tomato paste is lower in both sugar and sodium, so make the choice that's best for you.

**PER SERVING:** Calories: 452; Total fat: 4g; Protein: 75g; Sodium: 2,242mg; Fiber: 11g

# HOPPIN' JOHN

This Southern specialty, also known as Carolina peas and rice, is thought to bring good luck and prosperity when eaten on New Year's Day. The kale in this variation adds additional wealth—both because it's the color of American currency and because it's great for your health. It tastes delicious with some sautéed slices of vegan sausage. **SERVINGS: 4**

GLUTEN-FREE
SOY-FREE
NUT-FREE
BUDGET-FRIENDLY

3 (15-ounce) cans black-eyed
    peas, drained and rinsed
1 (14.5-ounce) can Cajun-style
    stewed tomatoes,
    with juice
2 cups hot water
1 cup stemmed and
    chopped kale
¾ cup finely diced red
    bell pepper
½ cup sliced scallions
1 medium jalapeño pepper,
    seeded and minced
1 teaspoon minced garlic
    (2 cloves)
1½ teaspoons hot sauce
1 vegetable bouillon cube
Cooked rice, for serving

PREP TIME: 15 MINUTES
COOK TIME: 4 TO 6 HOURS

1. Combine the black-eyed peas, tomatoes, hot water, kale, bell pepper, scallions, jalapeño, garlic, hot sauce, and bouillon cube in a slow cooker. Stir to combine.

2. Cover and cook on low for 4 to 6 hours.

3. Serve over cooked rice.

**INGREDIENT VARIATION:** If you can't find Cajun-style stewed tomatoes, you can use regular canned tomatoes and 1 tablespoon Cajun spice.

**LOVE YOUR LEFTOVERS:** You'll need to slice about 4 or 5 scallions to yield ½ cup. If you have any extra, use them to garnish this dish.

PER SERVING: Calories: 164; Total fat: 2g; Protein: 10g; Sodium: 250mg; Fiber: 8g

# AFRICAN SWEET POTATO STEW

This colorful and fragrant African Sweet Potato Stew is great garnished with crushed peanuts and lime. It's a hearty meal with an explosion of different flavors and lots of protein—perfect for a chilly fall evening. **SERVINGS: 4**

GLUTEN-FREE
SOY-FREE
BUDGET-FRIENDLY

4 cups peeled diced
    sweet potatoes
1 (15-ounce) can red kidney
    beans, drained and rinsed
1 (14.5-ounce) can diced
    tomatoes, drained
1 cup diced red bell pepper
2 cups Very Easy Vegetable
    Broth (page 14) or
    store bought
1 medium yellow
    onion, chopped
1 (4.5-ounce) can chopped
    green chiles, drained
1 teaspoon minced garlic
    (2 cloves)
1½ teaspoons ground ginger
1 teaspoon ground cumin
4 tablespoons creamy
    peanut butter
Pinch salt
Freshly ground black pepper

PREP TIME: 15 MINUTES
COOK TIME: 7 TO 8 HOURS

1. Combine the sweet potatoes, kidney beans, diced tomatoes, bell pepper, vegetable broth, onion, green chiles, garlic, ginger, and cumin in a slow cooker. Mix well.

2. Cover and cook on low for 7 to 8 hours.

3. Ladle a little of the soup into a small bowl and mix in the peanut butter, then pour the mixture back into the stew.

4. Season with salt and pepper. Mix well and serve.

PER SERVING: Calories: 514; Total fat: 10g; Protein: 22g; Sodium: 649mg; Fiber: 17g

# SWEET-AND-SOUR TEMPEH

This recipe is adapted from Kathy Hester's blog, *Healthy Slow Cooking*. Her recipes are easy and flavorful, and best of all, very quick to make. This Sweet-and-Sour Tempeh is a recent favorite with an explosion of different flavors I'm sure you'll love. SERVINGS: 4

NUT-FREE
BUDGET-FRIENDLY

PREP TIME: 15 MINUTES
COOK TIME: 7 TO 8 HOURS

FOR THE SAUCE

¾ cup fresh or canned
    pineapple chunks
½ cup crushed tomatoes
½ cup water
¼ cup chopped onion
¼ cup soy sauce
2 tablespoons rice vinegar
¼ teaspoon red pepper flakes
1 (½-inch) piece fresh
    ginger, peeled

FOR THE TEMPEH

2 (8-ounce) packages tempeh,
    cut into cubes
2 cups diced bell pepper
1½ cups diced pineapple
½ cup diced onion
Cooked rice, for serving

**TO MAKE THE SAUCE**

Put the pineapple chunks, crushed tomatoes, water, onion, soy sauce, rice vinegar, red pepper flakes, and ginger in a blender; blend until smooth.

**TO MAKE THE TEMPEH**

1. Combine the sauce, tempeh, bell pepper, diced pineapple, and onion in a slow cooker; stir well.

2. Cover and cook on low for 7 to 8 hours.

3. Serve over cooked rice.

**PER SERVING:** Calories: 324; Total fat: 13g; Protein: 24g; Sodium: 974mg; Fiber: 4g

# JACKFRUIT COCHINITA PIBIL

These tacos are ridiculously good. I've never eaten cochinita pibil made with the usual pork, but my friend Genaro blew me away with the jackfruit version when I was visiting him. I was taking a taco tour of LA (eating tacos at every restaurant), and his were by far the best in town. Here's hoping I did them justice! SERVINGS: 4

GLUTEN-FREE
SOY-FREE
NUT-FREE
BUDGET-FRIENDLY

2 (20-ounce) cans
    jackfruit, drained, hard
    pieces discarded
⅔ cup freshly squeezed
    lemon juice
⅓ cup orange juice
2 habanero peppers, seeded
    and chopped
2 tablespoons achiote paste
2 teaspoons ground cumin
2 teaspoons smoked paprika
2 teaspoons chili powder
2 teaspoons ground coriander
Pinch salt
Freshly ground black pepper
Warmed corn tortillas,
    for serving

PREP TIME: 15 MINUTES
COOK TIME: 8 HOURS

1. Combine the jackfruit, lemon juice, orange juice, habanero peppers, achiote paste, cumin, smoked paprika, chili powder, and coriander in a slow cooker; mix well.

2. Cover and cook on low for 8 hours or on high for 4 hours.

3. Use two forks to pull the jackfruit apart into shreds. Season with salt and pepper.

4. Heat tortillas directly over a gas fire, or in a skillet over medium heat for about 1 minute per side. Spoon the jackfruit into the tortillas and serve.

**INGREDIENT TIP:** A pickled onion garnish is definitely worth trying with this dish! To make one, bring ½ cup red wine vinegar to a boil in a small saucepan, then add 2 red onions, cut into rings. Reduce the heat to medium low and simmer until tender. Serve warm or cold, and store any leftovers in a jar in the refrigerator for up to a week.

PER SERVING: Calories: 297; Total fat: 2g; Protein: 5g; Sodium: 71mg; Fiber: 6g

# DELIGHTFUL DAL

Dal is a highly popular food from the Indian subcontinent, where the name can be used to describe a dish like this or the pulses used. It's the perfect midweek, easy-to-throw-together meal. **SERVINGS: 4**

GLUTEN-FREE
SOY-FREE
NUT-FREE
BUDGET-FRIENDLY

**3 cups red lentils, rinsed**

**6 cups water**

**1 (28-ounce) can diced tomatoes, with juice**

**1 small yellow onion, diced**

**2½ teaspoons minced garlic (5 cloves)**

**1 (1-inch) piece fresh ginger, peeled and minced**

**1 tablespoon ground turmeric**

**2 teaspoons ground cumin**

**1½ teaspoons ground cardamom**

**1½ teaspoons whole mustard seeds**

**1 teaspoon fennel seeds**

**1 bay leaf**

**1 teaspoon salt**

**¼ teaspoon freshly ground black pepper**

PREP TIME: 15 MINUTES
COOK TIME: 7 TO 9 HOURS

1. Combine the lentils, water, diced tomatoes, onion, garlic, ginger, turmeric, cumin, cardamom, mustard seeds, fennel seeds, bay leaf, salt, and pepper in a slow cooker; mix well.

2. Cover and cook on low for 7 to 9 hours or on high for 4 to 6 hours.

3. Remove the bay leaf, and serve.

**PER SERVING:** Calories: 585; Total fat: 4g; Protein: 40g; Sodium: 616mg; Fiber: 48g

# MOROCCAN CHICKPEA STEW

The complex and exotic fragrances of this dish make it especially pleasing and comforting to arrive home to after a long day of work. For some extra good nutrition and color in your soup, throw in some kale or spinach. **SERVINGS: 4**

SOY-FREE
NUT-FREE
BUDGET-FRIENDLY

1 small butternut squash,
    peeled and chopped into
    bite-size pieces
3 cups Very Easy Vegetable
    Broth (page 14) or
    store bought
1 medium yellow onion, diced
1 bell pepper, diced
1 (15-ounce) can chickpeas,
    drained and rinsed
1 (14.5-ounce) can
    tomato sauce
¾ cup brown lentils, rinsed
1½ teaspoons minced garlic
    (3 cloves)
1½ teaspoons ground ginger
1½ teaspoons ground turmeric
1½ teaspoons ground cumin
1 teaspoon ground cinnamon
¾ teaspoon smoked paprika
½ teaspoon salt
1 (8-ounce) package fresh
    udon noodles
Freshly ground black pepper

PREP TIME: 15 MINUTES
COOK TIME: 6 TO 8 HOURS

1. Combine the butternut squash, vegetable broth, onion, bell pepper, chickpeas, tomato sauce, brown lentils, garlic, ginger, turmeric, cumin, cinnamon, smoked paprika, and salt in a slow cooker. Mix well.

2. Cover and cook 6 to 8 hours on low or 3 to 4 hours on high. In the last 10 minutes of cooking, add the noodles.

3. Season with pepper, and serve.

**INGREDIENT TIP:** Save prep time by purchasing frozen or pre-cut butternut squash. Use 3 cups pre-prepped squash for this recipe.

**PER SERVING:** Calories: 427; Total fat: 4g; Protein: 26g; Sodium: 1,423mg; Fiber: 24g

# TEX-MEX TACO FILLING

Tacos are the greatest food ever invented. I love how endlessly my creativity can flow while crafting the perfect taco. Lentils and quinoa are my protein-packed ingredient of choice for this tasty Tex-Mex taco filling. Pile on the toppings and enjoy! SERVINGS: 4

GLUTEN-FREE
SOY-FREE
NUT-FREE
BUDGET-FRIENDLY

2 cups Very Easy Vegetable
    Broth (page 14) or
    store bought
1 cup green lentils, rinsed
½ cup uncooked
    quinoa, rinsed
¼ cup finely diced
    yellow onion
1½ teaspoons minced garlic
    (3 cloves)
2 teaspoons ground cumin
1 teaspoon chili powder
½ teaspoon smoked paprika
Pinch salt
Freshly ground black pepper
Tortillas or taco shells,
    for serving
Optional toppings: Nacho
    Cheese (page 125),
    Guacamole (page 127),
    minced onions, sliced
    radishes, cilantro, or
    hot sauce

PREP TIME: 15 MINUTES
COOK TIME: 7 TO 8 HOURS

1. Combine the vegetable broth, lentils, quinoa, onion, garlic, cumin, chili powder, and smoked paprika in a slow cooker. Mix well.

2. Cover and cook on low for 7 to 8 hours.

3. Season with salt and pepper.

4. Serve with tortillas or taco shells and your choice of toppings.

**PER SERVING:** Calories: 283; Total fat: 3g; Protein: 14g; Sodium: 434mg; Fiber: 17g

# RATATOUILLE

The first time I made Ratatouille (pronounced "rat-tuh-TOO-ee"), I was visiting my best friend in a quaint little town called Aix-en-Provence in southern France. There were farm stands on every corner, and I remember being impressed with the emphasis the French placed on fresh food. Here's my easy version of the meal we made. SERVINGS: 4

GLUTEN-FREE
SOY-FREE
NUT-FREE
BUDGET-FRIENDLY

3 cups peeled diced eggplant
1 medium yellow onion, thinly sliced
1 green bell pepper, cut into strips
1 red bell pepper, cut into strips
3 medium zucchini, sliced
2 teaspoons minced garlic (4 cloves)
1½ (28-ounce) cans plum tomatoes, drained
3 tablespoons tomato paste
2½ tablespoons olive oil
Pinch salt, plus more for salting eggplant
Freshly ground black pepper
½ cup chopped fresh basil, for garnish

PREP TIME: 15 MINUTES
COOK TIME: 6 HOURS

1. Put the diced eggplant in a colander over the sink, sprinkle with salt, and set aside.

2. Put the onion, bell peppers, zucchini, and garlic in a slow cooker. Pat the eggplant dry and stir it into the slow cooker.

3. Add the tomatoes, tomato paste, and olive oil to the slow cooker and mix thoroughly.

4. Cover and cook on low for 6 hours.

5. Season with salt and pepper. Garnish with the basil and serve.

**INGREDIENT VARIATION:** Up the protein in this dish by adding a can of drained and rinsed chickpeas (or your favorite canned bean). Want an extra kick? Stir in 1 to 2 tablespoons red wine vinegar.

**LOVE YOUR LEFTOVERS:** Freeze the remaining plum tomatoes in a freezer bag. Add them to Marinara Sauce (page 13) or soup.

PER SERVING: Calories: 226; Total fat: 10g; Protein: 7g; Sodium: 85mg; Fiber: 7g

# CAULIFLOWER BOLOGNESE

Dig out your food processor and let it do all the work prepping this meal for you. If you don't have one, you can get one online for about $20, or shop thrift stores for a high-quality model at an even lower price. It will quickly pay off in prep time saved. SERVINGS: 4

GLUTEN-FREE
SOY-FREE
NUT-FREE
BUDGET-FRIENDLY

½ head cauliflower, cut
    into florets
1 (8- to 10-ounce) container
    button mushrooms
1 small yellow onion,
    quartered
2 medium carrots, scrubbed
    and cut into chunks
2 cups eggplant chunks
2½ teaspoons minced garlic
    (5 cloves)
2 (28-ounce) cans
    crushed tomatoes
2 tablespoons tomato paste
2 tablespoons cane sugar or
    agave nectar
2 tablespoons balsamic vinegar
2 tablespoons
    nutritional yeast
1½ tablespoons dried oregano
1½ tablespoons dried basil
1½ teaspoons chopped
    fresh rosemary leaves
Pinch salt
Freshly ground black pepper

PREP TIME: 15 MINUTES
COOK TIME: 8 TO 9 HOURS

1. In a food processor, pulse the cauliflower, mushrooms, onion, carrots, eggplant, and garlic, until all the vegetables are finely chopped. Transfer to a slow cooker.

2. Add the crushed tomatoes, tomato paste, cane sugar, balsamic vinegar, nutritional yeast, oregano, basil, and rosemary to the slow cooker; mix well.

3. Cover and cook on low for 8 to 9 hours or on high for 4 to 5 hours.

4. Season with salt and pepper, and serve.

PER SERVING: Calories: 281; Total fat: 10g; Protein: 17g; Sodium: 855mg; Fiber: 20g

# KUNG-PAO TOFU

If I know I have an extra-busy morning ahead, I like to prep my marinade and chop my veggies the night before I make this spicy, saucy tofu dish. That way, when things are chaotic, I just need to throw all the ingredients into the slow cooker, turn it on, and head out the door. SERVINGS: 4

NUT-FREE
BUDGET-FRIENDLY

PREP TIME: 15 MINUTES
COOK TIME: 6 TO 8 HOURS

2½ teaspoons minced garlic (5 cloves)

1 tablespoon grated fresh ginger

1½ cups water

¼ cup soy sauce

¼ cup rice vinegar

¼ teaspoon toasted sesame oil

1 tablespoon sweetener

2 tablespoons vegetable bouillon (or 2 bouillon cubes, crushed)

1 to 2 tablespoons red pepper flakes

Pinch Chinese five-spice powder (optional)

1 (16-ounce) package extra-firm tofu, diced and pressed to remove excess water

4 large bell peppers, seeded and diced

2½ cups diced button mushrooms

1 (8-ounce) can water chestnuts, drained and diced

2 tablespoons cornstarch

1. In a bowl, combine the garlic, ginger, water, soy sauce, rice vinegar, sesame oil, sweetener, bouillon, red pepper flakes, and five-spice powder (if using). Set aside.

2. Combine the tofu, bell peppers, mushrooms, and water chestnuts in a slow cooker. Stir in the marinade.

3. Cover and cook on low for 5½ to 7½ hours.

4. Thirty minutes before serving, pour a ladle of broth into a cup and mix in the cornstarch. Pour it back into the slow cooker.

5. Cook on high for another 30 minutes.

**PER SERVING:** Calories: 280; Total fat: 6g; Protein: 15g; Sodium: 1,236mg; Fiber: 4g

# SOYRIZO ENCHILADA CHILI

This is a perfect dish to bring to a potluck. Everyone usually loves it, and if you're vegan, it ensures you have something substantial to eat at the party. You can top with a dollop of vegan sour cream and some freshly chopped cilantro. This one is definitely a party hit! SERVINGS: 4

NUT-FREE
BUDGET-FRIENDLY

PREP TIME: 15 MINUTES
COOK TIME: 6 TO 7 HOURS

3 (15-ounce) cans beans, drained and rinsed

1 (10-ounce) package frozen butternut squash

1 (10-ounce) can enchilada sauce

1 bell pepper, diced

½ medium yellow onion, diced

½ package soy chorizo, chopped

½ cup frozen corn

1. Combine the beans, butternut squash, enchilada sauce, bell pepper, onion, soy chorizo, and corn in a slow cooker; mix thoroughly.

2. Cover and cook on low for 6 to 7 hours or on high for 4 to 5 hours.

**INGREDIENT VARIATION:** If you're gluten-free, you can replace the soy chorizo with extra-firm tofu that's drained, pressed, crumbled, and sautéed with onion, garlic, and taco seasonings.

PER SERVING: Calories: 809; Total fat: 7g; Protein: 49g; Sodium: 645mg; Fiber: 46g

# ITALIAN TEMPEH

Tempeh is a widely used meat alternative that originated in Indonesia. A soy product made through natural culturing and fermentation, it's similar to tofu in the way it soaks up the flavors you cook it with, especially this Italian marinade. **SERVINGS: 4**

GLUTEN-FREE
NUT-FREE
BUDGET-FRIENDLY

**FOR THE MARINADE**
⅔ cup canola oil
¼ cup white vinegar
2 tablespoons water
2 tablespoons chopped
    fresh oregano
1 tablespoon garlic salt
1 tablespoon dried parsley
1 tablespoon agave nectar
2 teaspoons minced
    dried onion
1½ teaspoons dried basil
1 teaspoon freshly ground
    black pepper

**FOR THE TEMPEH**
1 (28-ounce) can
    stewed tomatoes
2 (8-ounce) packages tempeh,
    cut into cubes
1 red bell pepper, thinly sliced
1 green bell pepper,
    thinly sliced
1 red onion, thinly sliced

PREP TIME: 15 MINUTES
COOK TIME: 6 TO 8 HOURS

**TO MAKE THE MARINADE**
Combine the canola oil, white vinegar, water, oregano, garlic salt, dried parsley, agave nectar, onion, dried basil, and black pepper in a bowl; mix thoroughly.

**TO MAKE THE TEMPEH**
1. Put the stewed tomatoes, tempeh cubes, bell peppers, and onion in a slow cooker; mix well. Pour the marinade on top.

2. Cover and cook on low for 6 to 8 hours.

**INGREDIENT VARIATION:** If you don't have time to make the marinade, buy a vegan Italian dressing to use instead. I recommend Just Italian dressing from Hampton Creek.

**PER SERVING:** Calories: 345; Total fat: 20g; Protein: 24g; Sodium: 604mg; Fiber: 4g

# GUMBO

Gumbo isn't just a tasty stew—it's also the official state dish of Louisiana. There are many variations that include different seasoning blends, vegetables, and preparation techniques, but this one is the simplest. **SERVINGS: 4**

GLUTEN-FREE
SOY-FREE
NUT-FREE
BUDGET-FRIENDLY

1 (28-ounce) can diced
    fire-roasted tomatoes,
    with juice
2 (15-ounce) cans black beans,
    drained and rinsed
1 (16-ounce) package frozen
    sweet peppers and onions,
    or other stir-fry vegetables
2 cups frozen cut okra
½ teaspoon minced garlic
    (1 clove)
3 teaspoons Cajun seasoning
1 bay leaf
1½ teaspoons Tabasco sauce
    (optional)
Cooked rice, for serving

PREP TIME: 15 MINUTES
COOK TIME: 6 TO 8 HOURS

1. Combine the fire-roasted tomatoes, black beans, pepper-and-onion mixture, okra, garlic, Cajun seasoning, bay leaf, and Tabasco (if using) in a slow cooker. Mix well.

2. Cover and cook on low for 6 to 8 hours or on high for 4 to 5 hours.

3. Remove the bay leaf, and serve over rice.

**INGREDIENT VARIATION:** If you don't have Cajun spice, you can make your own by combining 2 teaspoons garlic powder, 2½ teaspoons smoked paprika, 1 teaspoon salt, 1 teaspoon onion powder, ¾ teaspoon cayenne pepper, ½ teaspoon red pepper flakes, ¾ teaspoon black pepper, 1 teaspoon dried thyme, and 1¼ teaspoons dried oregano. Mix it up and store it in a spice jar or plastic bag in your cupboard.

PER SERVING: Calories: 465; Total fat: 2g; Protein: 27g; Sodium: 72mg; Fiber: 23g

# MADRAS LENTILS

When I make a big batch of lentils at the beginning of the week, this is one of my favorite recipes to use them in. It's quick and easy, super flavorful, packed with protein, and very filling, especially when served over a bed of rice. SERVINGS: 4

GLUTEN-FREE
SOY-FREE
NUT-FREE
BUDGET-FRIENDLY

2 cups cooked Lazy Lentils
(page 24)
2 cups canned tomato sauce
or purée
1 large yellow onion,
finely diced
1 large russet potato, peeled
and cubed
½ cup canned unsweetened
full-fat coconut milk
3 tablespoons vegan butter
1½ teaspoons minced garlic
(3 cloves)
1 teaspoon ground cumin
½ teaspoon salt
½ teaspoon dried oregano
½ teaspoon ground coriander
¼ teaspoon red pepper flakes
Freshly ground black pepper

PREP TIME: 15 MINUTES
COOK TIME: 6 TO 8 HOURS

1. Combine the lentils, tomato sauce, onion, potato, coconut milk, vegan butter, garlic, cumin, salt, oregano, coriander, and red pepper flakes in a slow cooker. Mix well.

2. Cover and cook on low for 6 to 8 hours or on high for 3 to 4 hours.

3. Season with pepper, and serve over rice.

**LOVE YOUR LEFTOVERS:** Add the remaining coconut milk to a banana, kale, and berry smoothie, or use it as the base for an amazing dipping sauce.

**PER SERVING:** Calories: 398; Total fat: 17g; Protein: 16g; Sodium: 1,045mg; Fiber: 19g

# RICE AND BEANS

Since I love burritos, I thought it was necessary to include the staple burrito filling: rice and beans. Throw them in a tortilla with taco fixings, and you have a quick and easy dinner for the evening and lunch for the week. SERVINGS: 8

GLUTEN-FREE
SOY-FREE
NUT-FREE
BUDGET-FRIENDLY

Cooking spray or
    neutral-flavored oil,
    such as canola
4 cups uncooked long-grain
    white rice
8 cups Very Easy Vegetable
    Broth (page 14) or
    store bought
1 (15-ounce) can your choice
    beans, drained and rinsed
1 (4-ounce) can diced
    green chiles
½ cup diced yellow onion
3 garlic cloves, minced
1 teaspoon ground cumin

PREP TIME: 15 MINUTES
COOK TIME: 6 TO 8 HOURS

1. Spray or oil the slow cooker insert.

2. Combine the rice, vegetable broth, beans, green chiles, onion, garlic, and cumin in the prepared slow cooker.

3. Cover and cook on low for 6 to 8 hours.

**INGREDIENT VARIATION:** You can also throw in a handful of frozen peas, corn kernels, or any other frozen vegetable you think would be good.

**TIPS FOR TWO:** Since this makes quite a bit of rice, use it throughout the week in different ways: top it with melted vegan cheese, salsa, and scallions for a quick lunch, or serve it over tater tots with a dollop of vegan sour cream and sliced avocado for a dish that I like to call "tachos."

..................................................................................

**PER SERVING:** Calories: 482; Total fat: 2g; Protein: 18g; Sodium: 829mg; Fiber: 6g

# MEXICAN QUINOA

You can eat this on its own or wrap it in a tortilla to make a burrito. When shopping for the enchilada sauce, be conscious of your preferred spice level. If you like very spicy foods, the hotter flavors go great with this dish, but if you have a low tolerance for spice, mild is good, too. SERVINGS: 4

GLUTEN-FREE
SOY-FREE
NUT-FREE
BUDGET-FRIENDLY

Cooking spray or
    neutral-flavored oil,
    such as canola
2 (19-ounce) cans red
    enchilada sauce
1 (10-ounce) package frozen
    cubed butternut squash
1 (15-ounce) can kidney beans,
    drained and rinsed
1 (14.5-ounce) can fire-roasted
    petite diced tomatoes,
    with juice
1 cup frozen corn
1 cup uncooked quinoa, rinsed
½ cup finely diced onion
1 small jalapeño pepper,
    seeded and minced
1½ teaspoons minced garlic
    (3 cloves)
1 cup Very Easy Vegetable
    Broth (page 14) or
    store bought
1 package taco seasoning

PREP TIME: 15 MINUTES
COOK TIME: 6½ TO 8½ HOURS

1. Spray or oil the slow cooker insert.

2. Combine the enchilada sauce, butternut squash, kidney beans, fire-roasted tomatoes, corn, quinoa, onion, jalapeño, garlic, vegetable broth, and taco seasoning in the prepared slow cooker; mix well.

3. Cover and cook on low for 6 to 8 hours or on high for 3 to 4 hours.

4. Remove the lid and allow to cook on high for an additional 30 minutes, until the liquid is mostly absorbed.

**INGREDIENT TIP:** It's important to rinse your quinoa to avoid it having a bitter taste. Quinoa contains substances called *saponins*, which the plant releases to protect itself from predators. If they aren't rinsed away, they can leave a bitter, soapy taste.

PER SERVING: Calories: 526; Total fat: 9g; Protein: 23g; Sodium: 2,314mg; Fiber: 18g

# TERIYAKI TOFU

I didn't enjoy eating tofu for the first five or so years I was vegetarian, simply because I didn't know how to prepare it. If you're a lazy cook like me, don't worry—I've found you can really use any kind of sauce in this recipe. The tofu will soak it up, and you'll be good to go. If you've never pressed tofu before, see BBQ Tofu (page 36) for instructions. **SERVINGS: 4**

NUT-FREE
BUDGET-FRIENDLY

PREP TIME: 15 MINUTES
COOK TIME: 6 HOURS, 45 MINUTES

2 (1-pound) packages of
    extra-firm tofu, drained
    and pressed
¼ teaspoon salt
½ cup teriyaki sauce
1 (8-ounce) package chopped
    fresh kale
4 scallions, thinly sliced

1. Place the tofu in one layer on the bottom of a slow cooker.

2. Sprinkle the tofu with the salt and drizzle with the teriyaki sauce.

3. Cover and cook on low for 6 hours or on high for 3 hours.

4. Add the kale, then cover and cook on low until the kale is just wilted, about 45 minutes.

5. Garnish the tofu and kale with the scallions and serve.

**TIPS FOR TWO:** Serve leftover Teriyaki Tofu with cooked rice and some stir-fried peppers and onions to make several meals for two out of this recipe.

**INGREDIENT TIP:** Don't have teriyaki sauce? Make your own! All you need to do is whisk together ⅔ cup low-sodium soy sauce, ¼ cup rice vinegar, 1 tablespoon cornstarch, 2 tablespoons brown sugar, 1½ teaspoons ground ginger, and ½ teaspoon minced garlic.

**PER SERVING:** Calories: 224; Total fat: 10g; Protein: 23g; Sodium: 1,581mg; Fiber: 3g

# QUINOA AND VEGETABLES

I realize that it's totally clichéd to talk about how great quinoa is, but . . . I really love how great quinoa is! It's so light and fluffy, and it doesn't make me feel crappy after eating way too much. In fact, it makes me feel healthy because it's a superfood full of protein, minerals, and antioxidants. SERVINGS: 4

GLUTEN-FREE
SOY-FREE
NUT-FREE
BUDGET-FRIENDLY

3 cups Very Easy Vegetable Broth (page 14) or store bought

1½ cups uncooked quinoa, rinsed

1 large yellow onion, diced

1 medium red bell pepper, chopped

1 small carrot, chopped

1 cup chopped fresh green beans

1½ teaspoons minced garlic (3 cloves)

¼ teaspoon freshly ground black pepper

PREP TIME: 15 MINUTES
COOK TIME: 4 TO 6 HOURS

1. Combine the vegetable broth, quinoa, onion, bell pepper, carrot, green beans, garlic, and black pepper in a slow cooker. Mix well.

2. Cover and cook on low for 4 to 6 hours.

**INGREDIENT VARIATION:** This recipe is incredibly versatile—you can swap the vegetables out for your favorites, or add in any additional veggies you've got on hand. Have some fresh veggies that are about to go bad? Throw them in!

**PER SERVING:** Calories: 302; Total fat: 5g; Protein: 14g; Sodium: 590mg; Fiber: 7g

# ASIAN-INSPIRED JACKFRUIT FILLING

Use this savory, spicy filling in a tortilla, rice-paper wrap, or lettuce wrap, paired with fresh diced vegetables like cucumber, sprouts, and bell pepper. You can also add crushed peanuts for texture and protein. **SERVINGS: 4**

NUT-FREE
BUDGET-FRIENDLY

PREP TIME: 15 MINUTES
COOK TIME: 4 TO 6 HOURS

**FOR THE MARINADE**
¼ cup soy sauce
¼ cup hoisin sauce
¼ cup rice vinegar
3 tablespoons toasted
    sesame oil
1 jalapeño pepper (seeded
    if you want the dish
    less spicy)
2 tablespoons minced
    fresh ginger
2 tablespoons agave nectar
1½ teaspoons minced garlic
    (3 cloves)
Splash hot sauce (optional)

**FOR THE JACKFRUIT**
2 (20-ounce) cans
    jackfruit, drained, hard
    pieces discarded
1 red onion, thinly sliced
1 orange, peeled and quartered
¾ cup sliced scallions
Pinch salt

**TO MAKE THE MARINADE**
Put the soy sauce, hoisin sauce, rice vinegar, sesame oil, jalapeño, ginger, agave nectar, garlic, and hot sauce (if using) in a blender or food processor; blend well.

**TO MAKE THE JACKFRUIT**
1. Combine the jackfruit, onion, orange, and scallions in a slow cooker. Pour the marinade on top and mix well.
2. Cover and cook on low for 4 to 6 hours.
3. Season with salt.

**PER SERVING:** Calories: 365; Total fat: 8g; Protein: 5g; Sodium: 594mg; Fiber: 7g

# MOROCCAN EGGPLANT

The first time I had Moroccan food, I was traveling in Europe. At the time, I'd had very limited experience tasting worldly foods, and I was blown away by the exotic blend of spices. In this recipe, I call for Moroccan spice blend, which can be found at many grocery stores. SERVINGS: 4

GLUTEN-FREE
SOY-FREE
NUT-FREE
BUDGET-FRIENDLY

1 large eggplant, cut into
    1-inch pieces
1 (28-ounce) can whole
    tomatoes, with juice
1 (15-ounce) can chickpeas,
    drained and rinsed
1 large yellow onion,
    thinly sliced
1½ cups halved baby carrots
1½ teaspoons minced garlic
    (3 cloves)
1 tablespoon Moroccan
    spice blend
2 teaspoons ground cumin
½ teaspoon red pepper flakes
Pinch salt
Freshly ground black pepper
Cooked rice, for serving
Chopped cilantro, for garnish

PREP TIME: 15 MINUTES
COOK TIME: 6 TO 8 HOURS

1. Combine the eggplant, tomatoes, chickpeas, onion, baby carrots, garlic, Moroccan spice blend, cumin, and red pepper flakes in a slow cooker; mix well.

2. Cover and cook on low for 6 to 8 hours.

3. Season with salt and pepper.

4. Serve over rice, garnished with a handful of chopped cilantro.

**PER SERVING:** Calories: 280; Total fat: 4g; Protein: 13g; Sodium: 94mg; Fiber: 17g

# SUNDAY STAPLES

# BANANA OATMEAL

I have four slow cookers (I know, ridiculous), and I think this recipe is best cooked in the type that has a built-in timer that turns to "keep warm" when it reaches your desired cooking time. I personally like my oatmeal on the softer side, but if you don't, I recommend cooking this dish for a shorter amount of time. SERVINGS: 4

GLUTEN-FREE
SOY-FREE
NUT-FREE
BUDGET-FRIENDLY

1 cup steel-cut oats
3½ cups nondairy milk
2 bananas, peeled and mashed
½ cup raisins
2 tablespoons brown sugar
2 teaspoons ground cinnamon
1 teaspoon vanilla extract
¼ teaspoon ground nutmeg
½ teaspoon salt
2 tablespoons flax meal
    (optional)
Optional toppings:
    chopped nuts or seeds,
    sliced bananas, dried
    fruit, granola

PREP TIME: 10 MINUTES
COOK TIME: 5 TO 8 HOURS

1. Place the oats, nondairy milk, mashed bananas, raisins, brown sugar, cinnamon, vanilla extract, nutmeg, salt, and flax meal (if using) in a slow cooker. Mix well.

2. Cover and cook on low for 5 to 8 hours, depending on your preferred texture—firmer to softer oats.

3. Serve garnished with your choice of toppings.

**INGREDIENT VARIATION:** If you don't have bananas, try this recipe with ¾ cup frozen berries, or 2 cored and finely diced apples or pears.

**INGREDIENT TIP:** The flax meal is optional, but if you have some on hand, I recommend adding it for the extra nutrients it provides.

PER SERVING: Calories: 706; Total fat: 53g; Protein: 10g; Sodium: 327mg; Fiber: 11g

# GOOD MORNING GRITS

Grits are an inexpensive staple of the South. They're made of ground corn and can be either savory or sweet. There are three common varieties: instant, quick, and stone ground. Stone-ground grits yield the best results, but quick grits will work in a pinch. This recipe provides the basic technique for making grits—if you're feeling creative, melt some vegan cheese on top, then garnish with nondairy sour cream and sliced scallions. SERVINGS: 4

GLUTEN-FREE
SOY-FREE
NUT-FREE
BUDGET-FRIENDLY

Cooking spray or
    neutral-flavored oil,
    such as canola
1½ cups stone-ground grits
6 cups water
2 teaspoons salt
4 to 6 tablespoons
    vegan butter
Freshly ground black pepper

PREP TIME: 15 MINUTES
COOK TIME: 7 TO 8 HOURS

1. Grease the inside of a slow cooker with cooking spray or oil.

2. Add the grits, water, and salt and mix well.

3. Cover and cook on low for 7 to 8 hours.

4. Remove the lid. Scatter the vegan butter on top. Use a whisk to stir the grits until they reach an even consistency and the vegan butter has melted. Season with pepper and serve.

INGREDIENT TIP: For extra-creamy grits, replace the 2 cups water with 2 cups unflavored, unsweetened soy or almond milk.

INGREDIENT VARIATION: Spice things up and boost the nutrition profile of this dish by mixing in spices like rosemary, turmeric, garlic powder, or paprika.

PER SERVING: Calories: 197; Total fat: 18g; Protein: 1g; Sodium: 1,503mg; Fiber: 2g

# BREAKFAST RISOTTO

This breakfast porridge is filling and super easy to make. Do as you would with oatmeal and top with your favorite nuts, seeds, fresh fruit, and dried fruit. If it's not sweet enough for you, feel free to sprinkle it with more brown sugar. **SERVINGS: 4**

GLUTEN-FREE
SOY-FREE
NUT-FREE
BUDGET-FRIENDLY

4 cups nondairy milk

1½ cups arborio rice

1 cup finely diced tart apples such as Granny Smith

⅓ cup packed brown sugar

2 tablespoons vegan butter, melted

2 teaspoons ground cinnamon

½ teaspoon salt

¼ teaspoon ground nutmeg

Optional garnish: dried fruit

PREP TIME: 5 MINUTES
COOK TIME: 6 HOURS

1. Combine the nondairy milk, arborio rice, apples, brown sugar, vegan butter, cinnamon, salt, and nutmeg in a slow cooker; mix thoroughly.

2. Cover and cook on low for 6 hours or on high for 4 to 5 hours.

3. Garnish with dried fruit (if using), and serve.

**LOVE YOUR LEFTOVERS:** You'll need about 2 medium apples to yield 1 cup for this recipe. If you have some extra apple, snack on it while you prepare this dish!

**INGREDIENT VARIATION:** For a lower-fat version of this breakfast risotto, simply omit the butter. If you don't have arborio rice or you want a porridge with extra protein, use quinoa instead.

**PER SERVING:** Calories: 937; Total fat: 63g; Protein: 11g; Sodium: 402mg; Fiber: 9g

# NACHO CHEESE

No more missing cheese. Throw this tasty nacho sauce in your burrito, put a dollop in your marinara pasta, serve it as a side with chips, or add it to your pizza. It seriously tastes great with everything. SERVINGS: 4

GLUTEN-FREE
SOY-FREE
NUT-FREE
BUDGET-FRIENDLY

2 cups peeled chopped
    russet potatoes
1 cup chopped carrots
½ to ¾ cup water
1 tablespoon freshly squeezed
    lemon juice
½ cup nutritional yeast
½ teaspoon onion powder
½ teaspoon garlic powder
1 teaspoon salt
¼ cup Super Simple Salsa
    (page 128) or store bought
    (optional)

PREP TIME: 10 MINUTES
COOK TIME: 15 MINUTES

1. Boil the potatoes and carrots until soft, about 15 minutes.

2. Put ½ cup of water into a blender, followed by the lemon juice, nutritional yeast, onion powder, garlic powder, salt, and salsa (if using). Blend until completely smooth. If the consistency is too thick, add the remaining ¼ cup of water to thin it out.

**LOVE YOUR LEFTOVERS:** Store leftovers in an airtight container in the refrigerator for up to 3 days. If it thickens when you reheat it, add a splash of water.

**PER SERVING:** Calories: 237; Total fat: 1g; Protein: 13g; Sodium: 724mg; Fiber: 11g

# MUSHROOM GRAVY

Gravy makes everything taste better, and this one makes things taste the best. Use it on mashed potatoes, or to bring extra flavor to roasted vegetables. It's especially compatible with Baked Potatoes (page 27). **SERVINGS: 4**

NUT-FREE
BUDGET-FRIENDLY

PREP TIME: 10 MINUTES
COOK TIME: 10 MINUTES

1 tablespoon oil
1 small yellow onion, diced
1 cup finely chopped
    button mushrooms
1½ teaspoons minced garlic
    (3 cloves)
4 tablespoons flour
1¼ cups water
1 tablespoon soy sauce
½ teaspoon dried oregano
2 bay leaves
Freshly ground black pepper

1. Heat the oil in a saucepan, then add the onion, mushrooms, and garlic. Sauté until the onions are translucent.

2. Add the flour and mix to form a thick paste.

3. Add the water, soy sauce, oregano, and bay leaves, and bring to a simmer over medium heat. Season with pepper.

4. Remove the bay leaves. Use a whisk to gently mix the gravy until it thickens. Add more water if you prefer a thinner gravy.

**LOVE YOUR LEFTOVERS:** You can store this gravy for up to 1 week in the refrigerator.

**PER SERVING:** Calories: 79; Total fat: 4g; Protein: 2g; Sodium: 230mg; Fiber: 1g

# THE GREATEST GUACAMOLE

Avocados are one of earth's greatest gifts to us. Not only are they magically delicious on their own, but when paired with some minimal fresh ingredients and spices to make guacamole, they go from great to greater. SERVINGS: 4

GLUTEN-FREE
SOY-FREE
NUT-FREE
BUDGET-FRIENDLY

2 large avocados,
    halved, peeled, and
    roughly chopped
Juice of ½ lime
2 teaspoons olive oil
¼ red onion, finely diced
½ teaspoon minced garlic
    (1 clove)
½ teaspoon ground cumin
1 tablespoon freshly
    chopped cilantro
½ Roma tomato, diced
Pinch salt
Freshly ground black pepper

PREP TIME: 10 MINUTES

1. Mash the avocados to the desired consistency in a medium-size bowl.

2. Add the lime juice and oil. Stir in the red onion, garlic, cumin, cilantro, and tomato, then season with salt and pepper.

**LOVE YOUR LEFTOVERS:** Chances are that if you're making guacamole to complement your meal, salsa would also be a great addition. You can use your leftover lime juice, onion, cilantro, and Roma tomato in a yummy salsa, like Super Simple Salsa (page 128).

PER SERVING: Calories: 233; Total fat: 22g; Protein: 2g; Sodium: 48mg; Fiber: 7g

# SUPER SIMPLE SALSA

I love how salsa is so versatile. This is my favorite recipe to throw together quickly, but you can try throwing in bits and pieces of all your produce to see how it works out. I'll include some ingredient variations below for you to try out. **SERVINGS: 4**

GLUTEN-FREE
SOY-FREE
NUT-FREE
BUDGET-FRIENDLY

2 cups chopped tomatoes
½ cup diced yellow onion
2 tablespoons minced cilantro
Juice of ½ lime, plus more for seasoning (optional)
1 jalapeño pepper, seeded and chopped
½ teaspoon ground cumin
Pinch salt
Freshly ground black pepper

PREP TIME: 10 MINUTES

1. Combine the tomatoes, onion, cilantro, lime juice, jalapeño, and cumin in a bowl; mix well.
2. Season with salt and pepper, and add more lime juice (if using).

**INGREDIENT VARIATION:** As I mentioned above, salsa is something that's fun to try experimenting with. You can make it a little sweeter by adding some diced mango or other fruit. If you like it spicier, leave in the seeds from the jalapeño, or use a hotter pepper like habanero.

**PER SERVING:** Calories: 25; Total fat: <1g; Protein: 1g; Sodium: 46mg; Fiber: 2g

# CASHEW CREAM

This tasty topping is packed with protein and tastes great. Use it on savory dishes like soups, pastas, and potatoes. Check out my tips below for ideas on how to dress it up—and how to turn it into a sweet garnish for vegan desserts. **SERVINGS: 4**

GLUTEN-FREE
SOY-FREE

1 cup raw cashews, soaked
    overnight for at least
    7 hours and drained
½ cup water
¼ teaspoon salt
Freshly ground black pepper

PREP TIME: 5 MINUTES, PLUS 7 HOURS FOR SOAKING THE CASHEWS

1. Place the soaked cashews, water, and salt in a high-speed blender or food processor; blend until completely smooth.
2. Season with pepper.

**INGREDIENT VARIATION:** There are many ways to spice up this basic recipe. My favorite is to add 1½ teaspoons lemon juice and a pinch of garlic powder. You can also change it up by adding a minced garlic clove, 1 tablespoon finely diced onion, or a pinch of your favorite herb or spice. You can even make it sweet by adding 1 tablespoon maple syrup or agave nectar, or 1 teaspoon vanilla or cinnamon.

**PER SERVING:** Calories: 197; Total fat: 16g; Protein: 5g; Sodium: 154mg; Fiber: 1g

# HOMEMADE HUMMUS

Making hummus yourself is so much better than buying it premade from the store. The freshness is unbeatable and it's significantly cheaper. Spread it on a veggie burger, or use it as a dipping sauce for falafel, pita, or raw veggies. SERVINGS: 4

GLUTEN-FREE
SOY-FREE
BUDGET-FRIENDLY

1 (14-ounce) can chickpeas, drained and rinsed
1 teaspoon minced garlic (2 cloves)
3 tablespoons tahini
2 tablespoons freshly squeezed lemon juice
½ teaspoon ground cumin
1 to 2 teaspoons extra-virgin olive oil, as needed
Pinch salt
Freshly ground black pepper
Pinch paprika, for garnish
¼ cup toasted pine nuts (optional)

PREP TIME: 10 MINUTES

1.  Place the chickpeas, garlic, tahini, lemon juice, and cumin in a blender or food processor, and blend until the hummus is smooth and creamy. For a thinner consistency, add olive oil by the teaspoon.

2.  Season with salt and pepper.

3.  Transfer to a serving bowl and sprinkle with paprika and pine nuts (if using).

**LOVE YOUR LEFTOVERS:** If you have any leftovers, keep them in an airtight container in the refrigerator for up to 5 days. Use them in a wrap or sandwich during the week.

PER SERVING: Calories: 273; Total fat: 11g; Protein: 12g; Sodium: 66mg; Fiber: 10g

# PRESTO PESTO

When basil is in season, I love making big batches of this pesto to freeze in ice-cube trays. I keep the cubes in a plastic freezer bag for easy meal prep over the next few months. You can use it as the sauce on your spaghetti or drop a cube into your favorite vegetable soup. To make it nut-free, simply omit the walnuts. SERVINGS: 4

GLUTEN-FREE
SOY-FREE

1 cup lightly packed fresh
  basil leaves
½ cup raw walnuts
¼ cup olive oil
1 tablespoon nutritional yeast
1½ teaspoons minced garlic
  (3 cloves)
½ tablespoon freshly
  squeezed lemon juice
Pinch salt
Freshly ground black pepper

PREP TIME: 10 MINUTES

1. Combine the basil leaves, walnuts, olive oil, nutritional yeast, garlic, and lemon juice in a food processor. Process for 1 to 2 minutes, or until creamy.

2. Season with salt and pepper.

PER SERVING: Calories: 219; Total fat: 22g; Protein: 5g; Sodium: 42mg; Fiber: 2g

# MANGO CHUTNEY

This is another recipe I love to make in batches while mangoes are inexpensive, and freeze for future use. It's great with grilled tofu sandwiches, in Indian-inspired meals, and on savory pulled jackfruit. SERVINGS: 4

GLUTEN-FREE
SOY-FREE
NUT-FREE
BUDGET-FRIENDLY

2 large ripe (but not too soft)
   mangoes, peeled, pitted,
   and diced
2 tablespoons freshly
   squeezed lime juice
2 tablespoons canola or other
   neutral-flavored oil
2 tablespoons finely diced
   red onion
1 teaspoon minced garlic
   (2 cloves)
2 jalapeño peppers, seeded
   and minced
¼ teaspoon grated
   fresh ginger
1 teaspoon coriander seeds
½ teaspoon curry powder
5 tablespoons light
   brown sugar
4 tablespoons white
   wine vinegar
1 teaspoon salt

PREP TIME: 10 MINUTES
COOK TIME: 20 MINUTES
TOTAL TIME: 2 HOURS, 30 MINUTES

1. Combine the mango and lime juice in a bowl, and set aside.

2. In a large skillet, heat the oil over medium heat. Add the onion, garlic, jalapeño, and ginger, and stir until the onion is translucent.

3. Add the coriander seeds and curry powder, and stir.

4. Add the mango, sugar, vinegar, and salt. Bring to a boil.

5. Lower the heat to a simmer and cook for 10 minutes, until the liquid thickens and the mango becomes sticky.

6. Remove from the heat and let chill in the refrigerator at least 2 hours before serving.

PER SERVING: Calories: 214; Total fat: 8g; Protein: 2g; Sodium: 589mg; Fiber: 3g

# PERFECT PEANUT SAUCE

I love this recipe because it allows me to be lazy while still enjoying delicious and nutritious food. It only uses one bowl and one mixing utensil, and it pairs well with minimal-effort dishes like roasted vegetables and noodles. It's low-effort, low-maintenance, and low-cost—but high in health and flavor. **SERVINGS: 4**

BUDGET-FRIENDLY

PREP TIME: 5 MINUTES

½ cup peanut butter

1 tablespoon toasted
    sesame oil

1 tablespoon soy sauce

1 tablespoon freshly squeezed
    lemon juice

1 teaspoon minced garlic
    (2 cloves)

¼ teaspoon red pepper flakes

¼ to ½ cup water

1. In a bowl, combine the peanut butter, sesame oil, soy sauce, lemon juice, garlic, and red pepper flakes. Mix thoroughly.

2. Whisk in the water, starting with ¼ cup, then adding more until the dressing reaches your preferred consistency.

**PER SERVING:** Calories: 225; Total fat: 20g; Protein: 8g; Sodium: 375mg; Fiber: 2g

# DELICIOUS TAHINI DRESSING

Tahini is a paste made from sesame seeds that has a consistency like peanut butter. It's essential in recipes like hummus, and makes a great base for recipes like this dressing. It's got a nutty flavor, and paired with the sourness of the lemon juice, the sweetness of the maple syrup, and the saltiness of the soy sauce, it manages to be complex and deliciously simple at the same time. **SERVINGS: 4**

NUT-FREE
BUDGET-FRIENDLY

½ cup tahini

3 tablespoons freshly
   squeezed lemon juice

1 tablespoon maple syrup

1 tablespoon olive oil

½ teaspoon minced garlic
   (1 clove)

½ teaspoon soy sauce

½ teaspoon ground coriander

½ teaspoon ground cumin

Pinch salt

Freshly ground black pepper

PREP TIME: 10 MINUTES

1. In a bowl, whisk together the tahini, lemon juice, maple syrup, olive oil, garlic, soy sauce, coriander, and cumin.

2. Season with salt and pepper.

**COOKING TIP:** Mixing tahini with lemon juice makes a delicious dressing, but the addition of acid to the sesame paste can cause it to seize or stiffen. If the dressing is too thick, mix in hot water by the tablespoon until it's pourable.

**PER SERVING:** Calories: 227; Total fat: 20g; Protein: 4g; Sodium: 114mg; Fiber: 3g

# CARING FOR YOUR SLOW COOKER

If there's one thing I've learned from being an avid thrift-store shopper, it's that slow cookers will last forever if you treat them well. I picked up my first Crock Pot from Goodwill for four dollars. It's burnt orange with brown flowers on it, so I can only assume that it's from the 1970s. After its decades of life, and its decade with me, here's how I keep it going strong:

1. When you're finished with your meal, remember to turn the slow cooker off and unplug it. If it's left on, your food may overcook or even burn.

2. Pack up your leftovers and let the slow cooker cool completely, then remove the stoneware insert, fill it with warm, soapy water, and let it sit. It'll be much easier to wash without dried food stuck to it.

3. Don't use abrasive scouring pads to clean your slow cooker. A cloth, sponge, or rubber spatula will usually remove any residue.

4. Never immerse the base of your slow cooker in liquid. Try to keep it as dry as possible.

5. To clean the base, use a cloth dampened with warm, soapy water to wipe it down. If you're going to spray it down, be sure to use natural products.

6. If you have a newer slow cooker, you can wash the stoneware insert in the dishwasher. The lid can also be washed in the dishwasher, or by hand with warm, soapy water.

7. For best results, fill the ceramic crock at least halfway when cooking to ensure even heat and keep food from overcooking or burning.

8. Like all ceramics, the stoneware insert cannot withstand dramatic changes in temperature, so let it cool completely if you're going to use cool water. Submerging hot or warm stoneware in cool water will cause it to crack.

9. Don't use metal utensils in your slow cooker. Use wooden, silicone, or heat-proof plastic utensils to avoid scratching the stoneware insert.

10. Show your slow cooker love and care, and it will provide you love and care in return for years to come.

# THE DIRTY DOZEN
# AND THE CLEAN FIFTEEN

A nonprofit and environmental watchdog organization called the Environmental Working Group (EWG) looks at data supplied by the US Department of Agriculture (USDA) and the Food and Drug Administration (FDA) about pesticide residues. Each year, it compiles a list of the lowest and highest pesticide loads found in commercial crops. You can use these lists to decide which fruits and vegetables to buy organic to minimize your exposure to pesticides and which conventional produce is considered safe enough to eat. This does not mean they are pesticide-free, though, so wash these (and all) fruits and vege- tables thoroughly.

These lists change every year, so make sure you look up the most recent one before you fill your shopping cart. You'll find the most recent lists as well as a guide to pesticides in produce at EWG.org/FoodNews.

## The Dirty Dozen

Apples · Celery · Cherry tomatoes · Cucumbers · Grapes
Nectarines (imported)Peaches · Potatoes · Snap peas (imported) · Spinach
Strawberries · Sweet bell peppers
(Kale/Collard greens · Hot peppers)**

** In addition to the dirty dozen, the EWG added two produce items
contaminated with highly toxic organophosphate insecticides.

## The Clean Fifteen

Asparagus · Avocados · Cabbage · Cantaloupes (domestic) · Cauliflower
Eggplant · Grapefruit · Kiwifruit · Mangos · Onions · Papayas · Pineapples
Sweet corn · Sweet peas (frozen) · Sweet potatoes

# CONVERSION TABLES

## Volume Equivalents (Dry)

| US STANDARD | METRIC (APPROXIMATE) |
| --- | --- |
| ⅛ teaspoon | 0.5 mL |
| ¼ teaspoon | 1 mL |
| ½ teaspoon | 2 mL |
| ¾ teaspoon | 4 mL |
| 1 teaspoon | 5 mL |
| 1 tablespoon | 15 mL |
| ¼ cup | 59 mL |
| ⅓ cup | 79 mL |
| ½ cup | 118 mL |
| ⅔ cup | 156 mL |
| ¾ cup | 177 mL |
| 1 cup | 235 mL |
| 2 cups or 1 pint | 475 mL |
| 3 cups | 700 mL |
| 4 cups or 1 quart | 1 L |
| ½ gallon | 2 L |
| 1 gallon | 4 L |

## Weight Equivalents

| US STANDARD | METRIC (APPROXIMATE) |
| --- | --- |
| ½ ounce | 15 g |
| 1 ounce | 30 g |
| 2 ounces | 60 g |
| 4 ounces | 115 g |
| 8 ounces | 225 g |
| 12 ounces | 340 g |
| 16 ounces or 1 pound | 455 g |

## Volume Equivalents (Liquid)

| US STANDARD | US STANDARD (OUNCES) | METRIC (APPROXIMATE) |
| --- | --- | --- |
| 2 tablespoons | 1 fl. oz. | 30 mL |
| ¼ cup | 2 fl. oz. | 60 mL |
| ½ cup | 4 fl. oz. | 120 mL |
| 1 cup | 8 fl. oz. | 240 mL |
| 1½ cups | 12 fl. oz. | 355 mL |
| 2 cups or 1 pint | 16 fl. oz. | 475 mL |
| 4 cups or 1 quart | 32 fl. oz. | 1 L |
| 1 gallon | 128 fl. oz. | 4 L |

## Oven Temperatures

| FAHRENHEIT (F) | CELSIUS (C) (APPROXIMATE) |
| --- | --- |
| 250°F | 120°C |
| 300°F | 150°C |
| 325°F | 165°C |
| 350°F | 180°C |
| 375°F | 190°C |
| 400°F | 200°C |
| 425°F | 220°C |
| 450°F | 230°C |

# RECIPE INDEX

# INDEX